At-Risk Students and Thinking:

Perspectives from Research

Barbara Z. Presseisen, Editor

A Joint Publication of
National Education Association, 1201 16th Street, N.W., Washington, DC 20036–3290
Research for Better Schools, 444 North Third Street, Philadelphia, PA 19123–4107

Copyright © 1988
National Education Association of the United States
Research for Better Schools

Printing History
  First Printing: October 1988

Note

The work upon which this publication is based was funded in part by the Office of Educational Research and Improvement (OERI), U.S. Department of Education. The opinions expressed in this publication do not necessarily reflect the position or policy of OERI and no official endorsement by OERI should be inferred. Materials published as part of the Aspects of Learning series are intended to be discussion documents for teachers who are concerned with specialized interests of the profession.

Library of Congress Cataloging-in-Publication Data

At-risk students and thinking.

  (NEA/RBS aspects of learning)
  "A joint publication of National Education
Association. . .Research for Better Schools. . ."
  Bibliography: p.
  1. Socially handicapped children—Education—United
States. 2. Critical thinking—Study and teaching—
United States. I. Presseisen, Barbara Z. II. National
Education Association of the United States. III. Research
for Better Schools, Inc. IV. Series.
LC4091.A92   1988   371.96'7'0973   88-29151
ISBN 0-8106-1483-9

CONTENTS

IN THE SHADOW OF SYBIL
AND PYGMALION: A PREFACE

We live in an age when to be young and to be indifferent can no longer be synonymous. We must prepare for the coming hour. The claims of the Future are represented by suffering millions; and the Youth of a Nation are the trustees of Posterity.

—Benjamin Disraeli, *Sybil*

You see, really and truly, apart from the things anyone can pick up (the dressing and the proper way of speaking, and so on), the difference between a lady and a flower girl is not how she behaves, but how she's treated.

—Bernard Shaw, *Pygmalion*

Once there were two men who wrote lovingly but critically about their resident country, England. One man, destined to become the nation's prime minister, worried about the great gap that existed between the rich and the poor in a newly industrialized society. His book, which he titled *Sybil,* was a study of haves and have-nots. The second author was a playwright and social critic. In the drama *Pygmalion,* which he crafted for the most sophisticated theatre since that of the ancient Greeks, he studied the language of and interaction between the rich and the poor, between the "two nations" of the prime minister's novel. His play recalled the legendary sculptor who carved an exquisite ivory statue and who, with the aid of a Greek goddess, breathed life into his beautiful creation.

Teaching thinking and at-risk students in the United States today may seem to raise issues far removed from the problems of England over a century ago. Yet the dilemmas presented in *Sybil* and *Pygmalion* may not be so different from the educational problems of a society on the threshold of a postindustrial economic age. The gap between the rich and the poor, not only in material terms but also *intellectually,* may be greater now than when Disraeli feared for Victoria's England. Similarly, in an era of school reform and change, the expectations set for students who must prepare to live in a competitive and interdependent world may require an educational transformation no less miraculous than the metamorphosis Shaw saw possible in the relationship between Henry Higgins and Eliza Doolittle.

At the heart of these comparative situations is the power of thinking. Two men of English Letters saw the relevance of good thinking to one's behavior as well as to one's place in society. In America today, learning to think critically by completing a formal education may be a prerequisite for both success and survival in life. The major question to be answered is, How do we provide a quality education for *all* our citizens, including those whose risk of failure is greatest, whose talents must be challenged and realized in the few short years of childhood and adolescence?

Recent literature on improved schooling makes numerous references to the notion that teaching thinking—with an emphasis on higher-order cognitive skill development—ought to be an educational goal for all America's school-aged students (Costa 1985; Sleeter and Grant 1986; Cuban 1987). For reasons rooted in international economic competition, global technological development, and changing demographic circumstances, educators suggest every youngster needs to develop his/her abilities to solve problems, to examine issues and ideas critically, and to invent or creatively design new materials and solutions. It seems what was once the province of the gifted and talented, or at least of the academic select, has become a necessity for the entire school generation facing the twenty-first century (Task Force on Education for Economic Growth 1983; Children's Defense Fund 1987; Comer 1987).

There is a great discrepancy between this new goal for schooling and current practice in America's classrooms. Many recent reports calling for educational reform suggest the gap between rhetoric and reality is enormous (Sizer 1984; Toch 1984). Few deny what ought to be the realized dream of schooling in a democratic republic; but lessons of history suggest we have been here before and not always with great success. What does it mean to teach intellectual development to a school population whose dropout rate exceeds 30 or 40 percent, or even 60 or 70 percent (Levin 1987; Wehlage, Rutter, and Turnbaugh 1987; Rumberger 1987)? How do American educators approach groups of students who have been treated as outcasts for over a century (Ogbu 1986; Scott-Jones and Clark 1986) or who cannot speak the majority population's language (Durán 1985; Cummins 1986), let alone share many of its values or experiences? Examination and discussion of these issues are the focus of this study. The theoretical and practical bases of teaching thinking, including higher-order cognitive processes, to so-called "at-risk" students are explored and clarified, so that more specific steps can be taken to translate this new goal into educational reality in the near future. What has already been attempted in interventions with similar students will also be examined.

The initial chapters are an effort to begin to understand the difficulties and to clarify the problems introduced by this new thrust in American education. If posing the problem is an important first step in resolving a long-standing educational dilemma, as many suggest (Brown and Walter 1983; Frederiksen 1984), then the task at hand is significant. Education problems are often not well structured; by developing a clearer vision, we may make such a complex issue as the cognitive development of at-risk students more accessible and provide some avenues for interested parties to pursue. There is no issue more critical to address in current American education.

The literature on low-achieving students in American schools forms a massive collection. Similarly, the documents on cognitive instruction and the teaching of thinking comprise a very large body of information gathered from more than half a century of theory, research, and practice in schooling. In order to focus on the most significant material, we formulated several questions which guided the research conducted in conjunction with this study:

- What are the larger issues that make teaching thinking a concern of current school reformers and of educators of disadvantaged youths?

- Who are the at-risk students in America's schools? Is this a new problem for our country, or is it a long-standing one that is experiencing recent significant developments?

- What do we need to know about at-risk students' cognitive, as well as their social and emotional, development and how that influences their achievement in school?

- How does research on teaching thinking and problem solving inform our understanding of at-risk learners?

- What issues are raised when we seek to teach thinking to at-risk populations? What concerns are raised for the preparation of teachers?

- What are the implications for instructional and curricular policy and practice in developing the thinking skills of at-risk youth?

The discussions that follow begin to answer these questions. The contributions of various educators seek to elaborate on the multiple issues raised and to explore solutions to one of the nation's most serious problems.

—Barbara Z. Presseisen

REFERENCES

Brown, S. I., and Walter, M. I. 1983. *The art of problem posing.* Hillsdale, N.J.: Lawrence Erlbaum Associates.

Children's Defense Fund. 1987. A *children's defense budget, FY 1988: An Analysis of our nation's investment in children.* Washington, D.C.: the Fund.

Comer, J. P. 1987. New Haven's school-community connection. Educational Leadership 44(6): 13–16.

Cuban, L. 1987. Schooling the at-risk child: Lessons for policymakers and practitioners. Paper presented at the North Central Regional Educational Laboratory Conference, Chicago. Photocopy.

Cummins, J. 1986. Empowering minority students: A framework for intervention. Harvard Educational Review 56(1): 18–36.

Durán, R. P. 1985. Influences of language skills on bilinguals' problem solving. In Thinking and Learning skills. Vol. 2, Research and open questions, ed. S. F. Chipman, J. W. Segal, and R. Glaser, 187–208. Hillsdale, N.J.: Lawrence Erlbaum Associates.

Frederiksen, N. 1984. Implications of cognitive theory for instruction in problem solving. Research of Educational Research 54(3): 363–407.

Levin, H. M. 1987. Accelerated schools for disadvantaged students. Educational Leadership 44(6): 19–21.

Ogbu, J. U. 1986. The consequences of the American caste system. In The school achievement of minority children: New Perspective, ed. U. Neisser, 19–56. Hillsdale, N.J.: Lawrence Erlbaum Associates.

Rumberger, R. W. 1987. High school dropouts: A review of issues and evidence. Review of Educational Research 57(2): 101–21.

Scott-Jones, D., and Clark, M. L. 1986. The school experiences of Black girls: The interaction of gender, race, and socioeconomic status. Phi Delta Kappan 67(7): 520–26.

Sizer, T. 1984. Horace's compromise: The dilemma of the American high school. Boston: Houghton Mifflin.

Sleeter, C. E., and Grant, C. A. 1986. Success for all students. Phi Delta Kappan 68(4): 297–99.

Task Force on Education for Economic Growth. 1983. Action for excellence: A comprehensive plan to improve our nation's schools. Denver: Education Commission of the States.

Toch, T. 1984. The dark side of the excellence movement. Phi Delta Kappan 66(3): 173–76.

Wehlage, G. G.; Rutter, R. A.; and Turnbaugh, A. 1987. A program model for at-risk high schools students. Educational Leadership 44(6): 70–73.

1. FOCUS ON THE AT-RISK LEARNER: AN INTRODUCTION

by Barbara Z. Presseisen

Why have at-risk learners become a central concern of American education, and how does the learning or nonlearning of such students relate to the task of teaching thinking in our schools? The reform movement in education that characterizes the 1980s has come to grapple with such significant issues. At the heart are the basic challenge to educate youth to live in a democratic society and the need to understand how all the citizens of such a society come to terms with the cognitive, social, and affective demands of modern living.

In 1983 the National Commission on Excellence in Education (1983) issued its famous report on American education, *A Nation at Risk: The Imperative for Educational Reform.* Following its publication, many critiques and discussions concerning American education appeared, but one universal criticism of the report was its lack of sensitivity to the plight of minority and poor children in the nation's schools. While many of its recommendations for improved education seemed fitting for middle class students, *A Nation at Risk* offered few insights to help restructure the learning of students who dropped out of schooling. In addition, it gave little attention to the multiple causes of failure that seemed to stymie the learning careers of students who remained in school in many of the nation's largest communities.

We have numerous reasons for bringing the learning difficulties of at-risk students into focus as a primary aspect of reform in our nation's schools. Our realization of the change occurring in American demography is one of the prime motivators. Hodgkinson's (1985) major study alerted the country to the growing diversity of its population and the impossibility of serving the broad socioeconomic range of the nation's citizenry through simplistic policies. Hodgkinson stressed the increased number of children entering school from poverty households, from single-parent homes, and from minority backgrounds. He emphasized the need to coordinate the abilities of the nation's youth with the kinds of employment likely to be in demand in an increasingly technological economy. His study raised the question of whether American education is geared to preparing students for the interdependent and complex tasks associated with the world of the next century.

11

Contemporary studies of technological change also emphasize that students need to master higher-level skills in their pursuit of education and employment. A recent governmental study (Snider 1988) projects that the proportion of jobs held by college-educated workers will grow substantially in the next decade. The report also suggests that improved efficiency and flexibility among employees need to be matched by the development of their creative capacities as well. The ability to use information and the skill to make decisions and solve problems are the heart of a computer-based economy, which some researchers (Zuboff 1988) see as transforming the American workplace. If at-risk students are to be part of this major transformation, they, too, must become skilled in the higher mental processes underlying computation. Traditionally conceived basic skills as the goal of universal education are just not enough. Educational reformers have learned that the mastery of essential skills—which enables *every student* to learn more formal operations—is a much more appropriate national educational objective.

The quest for achievement, another concern central to the reform movement, is of major consequence to at-risk students. Much of the impetus behind current reforms stems from the nation's disappointment with student performance on standardized national tests such as the Scholastic Aptitude Test (SAT) and the National Assessment of Educational Progress (NAEP) (Vobejda 1988). At the international level, assessments of students from the major industrialized nations in subject areas such as mathematics and science have, unfortunately, shown American performance to be similarly lacking. Coupled with the nation's anxiety in the face of global economic competition, the nonachievement of at-risk learners seems a double threat.

Most at-risk students have little experience with national or international test batteries. Maeroff (1988) suggests "many urban minority students have not the slightest clue of what it takes to attain academic goals" (p. 635). Current research on achievement in big city systems indicates that the record of student performance is dismal, particularly when combined with dropout statistics. Moore and Davenport (1988) studied one class from a Chicago high school; they found that after graduation, 53 percent of the original class lacked the basic high school credentials and failed to achieve the minimal skills needed to obtain most jobs with a future (p. 2). Unfortunately, they also found that there is reason to believe that such poor performance is the usual rather than the exceptional occurrence among the graduates of many urban high schools.

All is not lost regarding change in urban schools. Two areas indicate reform-inspired innovation has influenced the lives of many at-risk students. Oakes (1987) reports that five types of change have actually been widely implemented in urban districts, even though these changes may be in contest with potential new difficulties caused by such implementation (see Table 1). Changes in the ways American educators conceive of intelligence and learning also have influenced many class-

Table 1.
Improvement Strategies: Promise and Problems

Strategy	Potential Benefits	Potential Difficulties
Effective schools/ curricula/ teaching	• Focus on schools and classrooms as a source of improvement • Possible empowerment of local schools, teachers, administrators, etc. • More rigorous curricula and better instruction	• Overregulation • Narrow curricula and instruction • Failure to address students' special needs
Alternative delivery systems	• Provide models of effective programs • Provide staff autonomy; program flexibility • Build home/school connections • Richer and more rigorous curricula • Increased desegregation	• Research only small segment of students • "Creaming" effects • Compromise desegregation efforts • Focus efforts on "damage control"
Early childhood programs	• Prevent or reduce later need for remediation • Provide needed childcare	• Create developmentally inappropriate programs
Social supports	• Provide needed health and family services • Reduce dropout rates	• Mimic ineffective school practices • Alienate community
Partnerships	• Provide additional services and resources • Provide technical assistance • Provide students with incentives • Create new links between schools and communities • Provide political support for schools	• Lack firm basis for continuation • Reinforce traditional practices

Reprinted from Table S.1 (page viii) of J. Oakes, *Improving inner-city schools: Current directions in urban district reform* (JN–02), October 1987. The RAND Corporation, 1700 Main Street, P.O. Box 2138, Santa Monica, CA 90406–2138.

rooms. Citing the research of scholars such as Sternberg and Gardner, many of America's teachers have come to realize that all children are intelligent, and that teaching and testing must become concerned with the *kinds* of learning children can master rather than with *how much* they reiterate through simple recall (Presseisen 1985). Building on these constructive approaches to educating at-risk students, Oakes calls for a number of policy changes she believes can break the cycle of school failure, unemployment, and social disintegration. She maintains that urban education needs to employ the following strategies:

- Build capacity at local school sites.
- Provide school autonomy and flexibility in designing and implementing improvement plans.
- Take a broad rather than a narrow view of curriculum and instruction.
- Reorganize classroom teaching and learning to promote urban children's positive self-perception, effort, and school performance.
- Provide real-life incentives for urban children to achieve at school.
- Coordinate efforts with the self-interests of other institutions and agencies to provide social and economic opportunities beyond the reach of school. (Oakes 1987, p. ix)

Making the teaching of thinking a cornerstone of the at-risk student's school experience is central to successfully implementing many of the strategies advocated by Oakes. Similarly, many of the restructuring notions and priorities called for in a recent Carnegie Foundation report (1988) on the renewal of urban education require honest wrangling with the question of the intellectual development of low-achieving children. Suggesting that school leaders be more responsive to teachers' ideas, emphasize the significance of accountability, stress the importance of early childhood preparation, or address the need for a coherent and connected core curriculum makes little sense if an overriding objective for *why* these priorities must be achieved is also not realized. To strive to help *all* students become independent thinkers—and understand the importance of their own autonomy as builders of their own knowledge systems—is an objective that has come to be recognized by the reform movement of the 1980s. Teaching thinking lies at the heart of what schools do best—providing a sound academic education (Spillane 1988). American schools cannot solve all the ills of our complex society, but they absolutely must help all students develop the expertise to use their own minds. Such an outcome enables them to meet both the academic and the socioeconomic demands of modern life.

What considerations do we need to raise if thinking is to become a central aspect of the education of at-risk students? We need to discuss

14

the traditional topics of education: what does teaching thinking mean to the building of curriculum, to the provision of effective instruction, or to the development of meaningful assessments? That is what the contributors to this volume set out to discuss. If real change is to be forged in the growing population of low-achieving learners, then American education must get beyond the politics and the rhetoric so often found in the literature on at-risk students. It must come to deal with the significant issues that influence what happens not only in classrooms but also in the minds of students and teachers alike.

In this volume, Barbara Presseisen first examines the nature of American schools' at-risk population. She explores the history of the metaphor and then describes in greater depth the characteristics of some particular at-risk groups. She points out that deliberate theoretical understandings have played an important role in determining past efforts to improve American education. Three models are examined to determine their effectiveness in meeting the needs of at-risk learners. Implications drawn from research on the instruction of minority children are also considered. Presseisen then discusses the potential impact of teaching thinking to at-risk students. The significance of both cognitive processes and metacognitive processes to the teaching of thinking is examined. The concept of mediation and the role of the teacher as the mediator of learning, both aspects of particular importance to the instruction of at-risk students, are discussed. Special materials and specific programs for teaching thinking are presented, as are some of the research findings on such programs. Finally, Presseisen considers implications for the future.

Richard Durán focuses his study on the poor school performance of minority students, and particularly on the development of classrooms as social environments for learning. He draws on the assisted performance theory as a basis for understanding the meaning of teaching, and particularly relates that construct to Vygotsky's zone of proximal development. According to Durán, gradually constructing the student's independence of thought and practicing the metacognitive tasks of modeling and internalizing particular strategies for learning are key aspects for all students' development—and all the more so for the at-risk learner. Durán discusses the implications of the assisted performance theory for classroom instruction and teacher preparation. He further discusses its implications for at-risk minority youngsters and their progress through the multiple tiers of educational development.

In her chapter on restructuring the educational reform movement, Beau Fly Jones emphasizes strategically focused instruction as a major goal in improving the education of at-risk students. Grounding her position in the extensive research base, she cites many of the poor practices that have become traditional in America's classrooms—student

15

labeling, lock-step recitation, and low-level assessment instruments. She also analyzes why cooperative learning; reciprocal, paired, and team teaching techniques; and parallel instruction provide better management and more promising learning experiences for many students, and particularly for at-risk minority students. Jones asks what is required to restructure schools and teacher education, and places curriculum reform at the top of her list in order to bring cognitive instruction alive in American schools. She also sees university-school partnerships, as well as laboratory-school cooperation, as approaches necessary to change the very mission of education in American society. The optimism, the hope that there is a critical mass of public opinion bent on changing the way we educate lower-achieving youngsters, comes through in Jones's assessment.

Trevor Sewell's study focuses on the ways American schools assess youngsters and determine their placement and needs with regard to instruction and learning. Like Durán and Jones, Sewell finds that much needs to be changed if we are to successfully educate this growing student population. Sewell draws on two traditions for evaluating youngsters' abilities: the traditional intelligence testing model and the potential view of "dynamic assessment." Teaching thinking, he proposes, requires the more dynamic approach, particularly for at-risk minority youngsters who have different cultural, linguistic, and social experiences upon which to build. The great challenge, according to Sewell, is for the educational system to adopt the sound professional practices conceptualized to remediate both cognitive and educational deficiencies in today's youth. Some research findings that give promise of answering questions in this realm are beginning to appear. According to Sewell, it is incumbent upon school districts to pursue further information on teaching thinking that will guide their policymaking and program management, and ensure the continued progress of such youngsters.

Daniel Levine reports that many commonly accepted generalizations can now be found in the literature on teaching thinking to at-risk students. He reviews these generalizations and stresses the importance of consistent and constant mediation of such students' instruction. He draws a more global and interrelated picture of what improved cognitive instruction will require of professional educators. Levine notes that research on implementing thinking programs in schools cannot ignore the literature on the change process and innovation in education. This leads him to speculate about issues that ought to be examined while developing policy on the education of at-risk students. He revisits topics addressed in earlier chapters, such as basic skills, bilingual education, learning styles, school structure, and instructional planning, and offers a more general perspective on the larger problem. Levine also considers

16

some of the worries associated with teaching thinking to low-achieving students and hastens to warn educators eager for reform not to repeat the mistakes of the past by being too simplistic, failing to allow diversity of approaches, or neglecting ties to the world beyond the school.

In the last chapter Jill Mirman, Robert Swartz, and John Barell address the issues of teacher preparation and empowerment in teaching thinking to at-risk students. These authors indicate that we must consider much more than just curriculum, instruction, and assessment—the traditional topics of education—when introducing thinking into the school. The whole school, its climate and policies, needs to be considered, as do the nature of the student population and its aspirations for development and learning. The authors are wary of the proposition that teaching thinking is a remedy for all the ills of an educational system that has not effectively served disadvantaged youth. They provide an analysis of what empowerment of teachers really means in the restructuring of the school and draw on this critique to suggest what teacher preparation, in turn, must become.

In an era of reform, a new perspective on education for all students has been proposed and an alternate approach for those most academically at risk introduced. The contributors to this volume may help to generate the understandings that can make this new approach a reality in America's schools. Their discussions surely will cause others to think and reflect on circumstances in current American education. There is no better place to begin serious change.

DISCUSSION QUESTIONS

1. Did the original school reform reports address the needs of at-risk students? Why or why not?

2. How is the school population in the United States changing?

3. Is training in "basic skills" likely to prepare students adequately for the jobs anticipated for workers in the next decade or two?

4. How is the teaching of higher-order thinking related to changes being called for in urban classrooms?

REFERENCES

Berlin, G., and Sum, A. 1988. *Toward a more perfect union: Basic skills, poor families, and our economic future*. Occasional Paper no. 3. New York: Ford Foundation.

Carnegie Foundation for the Advancement of Teaching. 1988. *An imperiled generation: Saving urban schools*. Special Report. Princeton, N.J.: the Foundation.

Hodgkinson, H. L. 1985. *All one system: Demographics of education, kindergarten through graduate school.* Washington, D.C.: Institute for Educational Leadership.

Maeroff, G. 1988. Withered hopes, stillborn dreams: The dismal panorama of urban schools. *Phi Delta Kappan* 69(9): 633–38.

Moore, D. R., and Davenport, S. 1988. The new improved sorting machine. Paper presented at the Education Writers Association meeting, New Orleans.

National Commission on Excellence in Education. 1983. *A nation at risk: The imperative for educational reform.* Washington, D.C.: U.S. Government Printing Office.

Oakes, J. 1987. *Improving inner-city schools: Current directions in urban district reform.* Santa Monica, Calif.: Rand Corporation.

Presseisen, B. Z. 1985. *Thinking skills throughout the curriculum: A conceptual design.* Bloomington, Ind.: Pi Lambda Theta.

Sheekey, A. 1988. The reality of education reform. *Youth Policy* 10(4): 20–24.

Snider, W. 1988. New technology seen as charting two U.S. "futures." *Education Week* 7(34): 1, 16.

Spillane, R. R. 1988. Don't sidetrack schools: Education is what we do best. *The Executive Educator* 10(6): 16–17, 34.

Vobejda, B. 1988. Report finds American students dismal in math. *Philadelphia Inquirer*, 8 June, 3A.

Zuboff, S. 1988. *In the age of the smart machine: The future of work and power.* New York: Basic Books.

2. TEACHING THINKING AND AT-RISK STUDENTS: DEFINING A POPULATION*

by Barbara Z. Presseisen

> At-risk *is a term recently added to the glossary of American education. Being aware of its history helps us understand some of the theoretical assumptions that have been followed in developing school programs for our neediest youth. Who are the students considered at risk, and what kinds of approaches have been pursued in attempts to help them? Have these approaches worked? On the basis of this research, what guidelines seem to be emerging today for teaching minority children?*

Before we can begin to consider the problem of teaching thinking to at-risk students, we must examine who these youngsters are and what we know about their development and learning. Similarly, our understanding about interventions to educate them in the past, as well as currently, sets the stage for new endeavors and innovative treatments.

"AT-RISK"—ORIGINS OF THE METAPHOR

At-risk appears to be the latest semantic label American educators have attached to several groups of students who have experienced difficulty or, in fact, failure in their careers as learners. Historically, other category names have been associated with these same populations: culturally deprived, low-income, dropout, alienated, marginal, disenfranchised, impoverished, underprivileged, disadvantaged, learning disabled, low-performing, low-achieving, remedial, urban, ghetto, language-impaired, and so on. Obviously, each group label mirrors many concerns, and chances are we would have great difficulty in characterizing a typical member of any particular group (Rumberger 1987). Most often, students in all these categories come from poverty-stricken economic backgrounds. They are more prone to social and familial stress, characterized by a lack of control over their lives, by a dim perspective in terms of their future hopes, and by a limited view of their

---

*An earlier version of this chapter and Chapter 3 was presented in a position paper, "Teaching Thinking and At-Risk Students: Understanding the Problem," written for a cross-laboratory conference held in Philadelphia in November 1987. References for both chapters follow Chapter 3 in this volume.

own personal worth and self-esteem. Frequently, these youngsters are members of a minority group; they are racially, linguistically, or socially partitioned from the members of the mainstream or majority culture. They are a vulnerable underbelly of a complex, sometimes callous or naive society.

"At-risk" is a metaphoric expression that appeared with increasing frequency in the early writings of the current educational reform movement (National Commission on Excellence in Education 1983; National Coalition of Advocates for Students 1985; McDill, Natriello, and Pallas 1986). Rather than drawing on a religious orientation, as have many educational movements of the past—e.g., "the crusade of the 60s," "save the children"—at-risk connotes medical or epidemiological sources. The label suggests that populations of young people are being threatened by a systematic, external danger in the larger community. There is a fear that some growing menace is out of control; that a particular group may become infected; that unless we do something dramatic soon, young lives will be negatively affected for a long time, and the venomous impact will continue to spread. The parallels to substance abuse and AIDS infection seem more than coincidental.

But there is also a positive side to the at-risk term. Through proper treatments or positive interventions, at-risk students *can* improve; they can achieve success. The compelling problems are rooted outside the learner in the institutions that serve her/him, perhaps in the society itself. Risk can be mitigated by knowledgeable practice and informed understanding. The youngsters themselves can generate potential healing powers, if their instructors and the educational system encourage and facilitate their best performance. What students *do* needs to be separated from who students *are* and from the circumstances of their daily lives. Teachers can become mediators of educational excellence if they are willing to change their view of their mission—and of many students they teach (Whimbey and Whimbey 1975; Sternberg 1981; Feuerstein et al. 1985; Presseisen 1985). Teaching thinking to so-called at-risk youngsters is a challenge characterized by the metaphor's own dimensions.

GROUPS PARTICULARLY AT RISK

Who are America's at-risk students? They seem to be the daughters and sons of families whose maladies are interconnected and who fall prey to a host of disastrous conditions. The most visible at-risk population is that of dropouts, students who leave school as early as the law permits and without benefit of diploma or graduation.

Two pictures of typical dropouts are presented in the research literature:

The picture we have of the at-risk student is that of a young person who comes from a low socioeconomic background which may include various forms of family stress or instability. If the young person is consistently discouraged by the school because he or she receives signals about academic inadequacies and failures, perceives little interest or caring from teachers, and sees the institution's discipline system as both ineffective and unfair, then it is not unreasonable to expect that the student will become alienated and uncommitted to getting a high school diploma. (Wehlage, Rutter, and Turnbaugh 1987, p. 71)

The researchers found that a disproportionate number of dropouts were male, older than average for their grade level, and members of racial or ethnic minorities. They were likely to attend urban public schools in the South or West. They came from low-income—often single-parent—families; many had mothers who worked outside the home, who lacked formal education, and who had low educational expectations for their children. These young people had few study aids available to them at home, and their parents were not interested in monitoring their school or nonschool activities. They had fewer opportunities than their classmates for learning outside of school; their grades and test scores were lower; they read less, did less homework, and reported having more disciplinary problems in school. They also reported that they were unpopular with other students and alienated from school life. They tended not to take part in extracurricular activities, and they said that their jobs were more important to them than school. (Strother 1986, p. 326)

Although statistics on dropouts are often collected neither under consistent conditions nor according to a standardized definition, some guidelines seem applicable to understanding the general problems of this population across the country (Hammack 1986). Hispanic students, members of the fastest-growing minority in the United States, exhibit the highest dropout rate, followed by Blacks and whites. Black males have actually shown improvement over the past years in their propensity to finish high school (Rumberger 1987), but because the Black portion of the overall population is increasing, their national dropout rate continues to rise. Furthermore, the number of Black students applying to, attending, and completing higher education actually declined over the last several years (Hodgkinson 1985, p. 15).

That many students in large urban districts are dropping out comes as no surprise. Fine (1986) reports on a New York City senior high school in which only 20 percent of a class ultimately graduated from that building. The remaining students were discharged, transferred (and perhaps finished at alternate sites), moved out of the state or the country, received GED diplomas, went into the military, enrolled in private schools, or were never located at all. The Black and Latino students of that school exhibit a host of the "nested problems" suggested by Mann (1986) as common to the urban ghetto: for example, little relationship between schooling and future income for a young man destined to be a drug dealer; competition with social and family

21

obligations for a 16-year-old girl whose Lupus-infected mother needed the girl to care for her at home where "nobody speaks English good." One student interviewed (who scored 1200 on his SAT) critically chastised a teacher who disallowed class discussion and appeared to deride each student's viewpoint whenever it was given (Fine 1986, p. 396). Perhaps more disturbing are the reflections of many students who seem to accept dropping out as an everyday, humdrum thing to do, without immediate cause and in competition with no particular distraction.

> There is another group that leaves without a critical analysis of schooling or economic benefits, and with no immediate crisis. These adolescents leave school because they live surrounded by unemployment and poverty, have experienced failure in school and have been held back at least once, feel terrible about themselves, and see little hope. Most of their friends are out of school, also without diplomas. Their words speak mostly of disappointment over the promises of schooling that turned out to be a lie. (Fine 1986, p. 398)

And, lastly, there are the students literally thrown, pushed, or shamed out of the system by retention practices that keep some youngsters in ninth grade for as long as three years. All dropouts do not necessarily fit one common description.

Potential dropouts are, in fact, only the tip of the iceberg. Long before they turn sixteen or arrive at their sophomore year in high school, many at-risk youngsters have been evaluated as very underskilled in various content areas. Their most obvious weakness is reading difficulty. In a country, and a society, that emphasizes the significance of the written word in education, a student who is not proficient at decoding printed text is a first-order school failure. For a variety of reasons many at-risk youngsters, particularly Blacks and Hispanics, have not shared their classmates' success in learning to read well (Engs 1987). Even in the primary grades, their school performance is below standard, well behind that of white students in the same grades, and they never fully make up the difference (National Assessment of Educational Progress 1987). In addition, the ability to generate or infer meaning from text is frequently associated with learning to read well and is increasingly considered the heart of developing literacy (Perfetti 1984; Brown 1984). Poor readers fail to comprehend the meaning of much of what they read; they are not able to interrelate ideas suggested by the context of the written material, and they rarely correct their own errors.

> Poor readers compared with good readers show little evidence when reading of such learning activities as skimming, looking back, and other fix-up strategies. They fail to monitor their comprehension deeply enough to permit them to detect violations of internal consistency in texts or even of just plain

common sense. They rarely take remedial action even if an error is detected;
in short, their comprehension-monitoring is weak to non-existent. (Brown 1984,
p. 5)

If these deficiencies go uncorrected throughout a student's career, it is
not difficult to see why that student, burdened with below-average
reading scores, is twice as likely to drop out as are his or her classmates
who have achieved normal or above-average reading levels.

Elementary students whose mathematical performance is weak exhibit
some characteristics similar to those of reading deficient youngsters.
Russell and Ginsburg (1984) have found "their difficulties result from
such mundane factors as immaturities of mathematical knowledge (e.g.,
bugs characteristic of younger children), inattention, poor execution of
adequate strategies (e.g., mental addition), or lack of facility in dealing
with large numbers" (p. 243). In addition, researchers (Gannon and
Ginsburg 1985) have found social and emotional factors often influence
the learning of mathematics, compounding the problems of some at-risk
students who—because of disciplinary difficulties—find it almost impossible to master the developmental skills required by the subject matter.
In a world increasingly influenced by applications of mathematics in
technological employment, the at-risk student pays twice for the lack of
school success: once when she/he fails to acquire the mathematical
knowledge that class peers do, and again throughout the rest of her/his
working life, when more demanding jobs will be unavailable because
they require quantitative ability beyond what the at-risk student
possesses.

Youngsters are, of course, expected to acquire other content skills at
school besides reading and mathematics. Science, social studies, fine
arts, writing, and composition all require some ability to read or
calculate in order to comprehend the material. The significant point is
that continued failure to understand these important building blocks of
the school's program haunts the academic career of nonachieving
students, trapping them in a cycle of cumulative ignorance, and perhaps
setting them on the path to dropping out. Because they are uninspired
in their immature appreciation of the ideas of their culture, it is not
surprising to find truancy often characterizes the at-risk student's
involvement at school. And, further, the world outside the classroom
becomes a much more enticing distraction.

A third group of at-risk youngsters is comprised of those deemed
"disabled" or bona fide dysfunctional in a particular way and categorized as deficient, although seemingly educable. Disabilities in children
can result from numerous difficulties. For the purpose here of discussing
at-risk youngsters, we will highlight two such difficulties. Youngsters
suffering from dyslexia constitute one group, and those particularly

impaired because they cannot speak English, or speak it very limitedly, comprise a second so-called disabled population.

Dyslexia is a complex neurological condition that prevents the brain from receiving, storing, or expressing information appropriately. One noted psychologist estimates that a majority of the country's illiterates have some degree of dyslexia (Hochman 1987, p. 14). Probably due to influences in their prenatal development, learners with dyslexia agonize over tasks most students eventually take for granted: learning the alphabet, writing their own name, spelling simple words like *dog*. Many dyslexics go through school ashamed and confused because they seemingly cannot learn things that other children can, regardless of how able those other children might be. Many more boys than girls are dyslexic, and recent research suggests influence of the male hormone testosterone during the second trimester of pregnancy may account for their abnormal brain development (*New York Times 1987*).

As much as 15 percent of the American population may exhibit symptoms of various handicapping conditions akin to dyslexia. Many at-risk students are diagnosed as "learning disabled," or even "retarded," but are not treated for their dyslexic difficulties. Poor classroom behavior, low self-estimates of their own ability, and dislike of school commonly follow their initial unsuccessful start at learning, especially in reading and language comprehension. Hochman (1987) reports that a recent study of the National Institute of Juvenile Justice and Delinquency Prevention indicates that 36.5 percent of officially adjudicated delinquent boys were categorized as "learning disabled," and that many of their frustrations with schoolwork were rooted in dyslexic-based symptoms: poor language functioning, inability to read, stuttering or lisping, short-term memory difficulty, and even lag of maturity.

Students who do not speak standard English form another subgroup often included in at-risk populations. Of the numerous immigrant groups typically found in urban areas, Hispanic students far outnumber those from other non-English-speaking countries. They make up three-quarters of the students with limited English proficiency in American schools (Mezzacappa 1987b). Hispanic students generally attend school in America's largest cities and constitute healthy segments of those districts' student populations: over 30 percent in New York City, 45 percent in Los Angeles, 52 percent in San Antonio, 32 percent in Miami, 31 percent in Denver, and 35 percent in Hartford (Pifer 1979; National Commission on Secondary Education for Hispanics 1984). Hispanic students have the highest dropout rate of any minority population, and their families often live well below the poverty line (Mezzacappa 1987a; Church 1985; Cooper 1987). Hispanics are expected to replace Blacks as the nation's largest minority population before the middle of the next century.

Not being able to speak English obviously precludes students from being able to read or write it well. The lack of a common means of communication also hinders classroom interaction, especially if the instructor's command of Spanish is limited. Bilingual education, currently a controversial and political issue in the schooling of "language deficient" students, has been looked upon primarily as a means of correcting or compensating for student inadequacies. Some educational policymakers find the philosophy behind major programs for Hispanic youth has been wrongheaded and, to some degree, has even created a large part of the dropout problem faced today in the Latin American community.

Schools, as transmitters of society's values, in a variety of ways have made a signal contribution to the performance rates of Hispanics—by shunting Spanish-speaking children from poor families into educational tracks designed for low achievers, by classifying them as mentally retarded or emotionally disturbed, by denigrating their Hispanic heritage, by giving them the message that they cannot, or are not expected to, succeed. In short, the public education system as a whole has neither welcomed Hispanic children nor been willing to deal with their learning problems in any effective way. (Pifer 1979, p. 10)

American Hispanics are a predominantly young, family-oriented, and highly fertile population. Demographic estimates suggest that because Hispanics are the nation's fastest-growing minority, their role as an at-risk population presents unique problems for schools (Yankelovich, Skelly, and White 1984). Helping Hispanic youngsters acquire the intellectual skills needed to compete successfully in the American mainstream has a slightly different linguistic twist than does the challenge of other students' learning, but the fact that they are an at-risk group in need of assistance—sharing problems of poverty and poor performance—is nowhere denied.

This review of who America's at-risk students are suggests there is no simple way to describe this burgeoning population. According to many educational leaders (Olson 1987), the complex task of untangling the behavioral, cognitive, neurological, and social problems that plague nearly half the students in America's schools requires urgent and immediate attention. In the long run, the current school reform movement cannot ignore the needs of these youngsters and hope to succeed; neither can it pursue remedies such as higher academic standards, increased curricular requirements, and more stringent achievement testing if it does not at the same time radically transform the poor performance of at-risk learners. Central to that transformation is attention to their intellectual or cognitive-developmental needs. Levin (1986), as well as others, sees an impending national crisis on the horizon of our educational future: "the emergence of a dual society with a large and poorly educated underclass, massive disruption in higher education, reduced economic competitiveness of the nation as well as of individual states, and industries that are most heavily impacted by these populations" (p. 13). In short, at-risk students represent the threat of the failure of democratic society itself, the fear that we are creating, mainly in our inner-city neighborhoods, an ineradicable, untrained underclass plagued by a self-perpetuating pathology of joblessness, welfare dependency, and crime. This population is without a vision of the American dream. We may find it more comfortable to look the other way, but it is incumbent on us, as both educators and responsible citizens, to see that American schools address the major learning problems of this complex population. We will not complete such a task overnight, but our need to start immediately seems self-evident.

WHAT HAS BEEN DONE? WHAT HAS BEEN LEARNED?

Concern for the lack of educational success among disadvantaged youths has a long history in American society. Determining what practices work or actually resolve the complex problems facing at-risk students is not a simple feat. What explanations are current? According to several researchers in the field (Banks 1982; Ginsburg 1972, 1986), large, national efforts can be seen as historically based in at least one of three theoretical views.

The first theoretical view suggests at-risk students are unsuccessful in school because of their cognitive deficits; this inability to engage in conceptual learning results mainly from their genetic inheritance. Such a position stems from a theory that considers human intelligence an outcome of biological evolution, resting mainly on the existence of immutable general ability and based largely on studies of correlational data. This nativist approach, rooted in psychological research such as that begun by Jensen (1969, 1981, 1985, 1986) in the 1960s, proposes that one can expect only a minimal level of change in the cognitive development of lower class children—and of Black students in particular—and concentrates efforts on intervention programs involving drill and practice in basic skill achievement and on some positive social development activities. Grouping and tracking practices, primarily placing low-achieving students with like peers and segregating them from academically more successful students, were begun in the 1960s and were justified according to this initial approach. A rather narrow conception of remediation became the chief educational goal.

A second theoretical view, one stressing the environmental causes underlying poor students' cognitive deficits, was also developed in the 1960s. Rooted in the more liberal climate of President Johnson's War on

Poverty program and the Elementary and Secondary Education Act of 1965, one of its main thrusts is to alleviate cultural deprivation. Supporters maintain that lower class students do not do well in school because of family disorganization, poverty, minimal intellectual and cultural stimulation, and lack of experience in the ways of the more educated, sophisticated community. Cultural deprivation theorists stress the need for programs to compensate for these cognitive and intellectual deficits, and especially to open opportunities for learning and to emphasize basic skills through intensive, systematic, and behaviorally oriented instruction (Bereiter and Englemann 1966). During the 1960s large, national programs implemented the cultural deprivation view. Head Start, Follow Through, Upward Bound, and Project Literacy were typical of the attempts to provide access to learning and to apply the knowledge of social science to the needs of a program of "compensatory education which can prevent or overcome earlier deficiencies in the development of each individual" (Bloom, Davis, and Hess 1965, p. 6).

At the same time, another thrust of the environmentalist approach is to stress the importance of open access and the integration of minority youths into the mainstream community. Through desegregation efforts, urban students were transported across neighborhoods and even city limits to higher-status, racially mixed schools. Finding their justification in data from the report by Coleman (1966) and in further information provided through the U.S. Commission on Civil Rights, school districts launched massive busing programs in many American communities. These programs sought two goals: to prove that social class and racial identity could be constructive correlates of students' academic achievement, and to improve the racial attitudes and human relations skills of minority and majority students so that both could live more harmoniously in America's pluralistic society.

A third theoretical view, which is at least partly in conflict with the first two perspectives, emerged in the early 1970s. Researchers who emphasize cultural pluralism maintain that educational programs for minorities should be based on premises different from those that characterized earlier approaches (Banks 1982). These bicultural or multicultural theorists reject both the nativist perspective and the cultural deficits theory as biased or misguided and, ultimately, as wrong.

As Labov (1972) pointed out at the time, many of these studies—like those of Bereiter and Englemann (1966), and Deutsch (1967)—employed rigid methodologies and were not based on an understanding of children in general or poor children in particular. It is easy to get poor children to do badly on some standardized test; it is much harder to employ methods sensitive to their true competence. Anyone who has real contact with poor children, I felt, would realize that much of the psychological research was insensitive, narrow minded, and wrong. (Ginsburg 1986, pp. 170–71)

27

In essence, cultural pluralists propose that at-risk students fail to achieve in school not because they come from deprived cultures, but because their cultures are different from the school's culture. Most significant, according to this view, is the fact that American schooling has tended to ignore or deride students' cultures and has failed to develop teaching techniques or instructional strategies consistent with the learning styles, lifestyles, and values of the particular learners.

> Many Black children's problems in school stem not so much from limited cognitive abilities as from conflicting orientations as to the conditions and attitudes most appropriate for learning, as well as the difficulties involved in making the transition from the frames of reference and ways of behaving of the home to those of the school. Without conscious awareness of these differences, and the knowledge necessary to use them advantageously, cultural conflict between white teachers' and Black students' expectations are inevitable. (Gay 1975, p. 30)

Programs of the 1970s that emphasized the at-risk student's own cultural awareness and history were consistent with this third view of cultural differences. Bilingual instructional programs that sought to build a language bridge between Hispanic and Anglo communities were another programmatic response consistent with the cultural difference position (Cardenas 1986). Even the so-called "effective schools" literature, strongly rooted in the potential of a positive learning climate in successful schools, emphasized that the mutual respect the multiculturalists maintain necessarily precedes the clear communication and participatory collaboration of a meaningful educational effort (*Educational Leadership* 1982; *Educational Researcher* 1983; Edmonds 1986). This third approach stresses the bridging of different worlds as the basis for student learning.

Did the programs emanating from these three theoretical views succeed in terms of helping at-risk students? Outcomes are much more difficult to track than theoretical approaches. First, what exactly we hoped to achieve is difficult to determine. Did we want rising test scores or social outcomes? Did we want to prevent dropping out, reduce crime, or improve life skills? Did we want to advance English language skills at the expense of native language abilities? Did we want to prepare students to be better workers and, if so, for what types of jobs did we want to prepare them? Once we settle some of these issues, we are then faced with the methodological problems of finding answers in the overwhelming data that have been amassed by national programs over the past two decades.

As might be expected, research results on programmatic effects for at-risk students are somewhat controversial and frequently mixed. For example, a review of several interventions of Project Follow Through, which emphasized direct instruction, has found seemingly long-lasting effects on the achievement of various groups of inner-city youths, particularly in reading (Gersten and Keating 1987). However, these same reports reveal that the dropout rates in these populations continue to be persistently high, even when higher test scores indicate content mastery. In addition, the educational climate of many of the participating schools seems little improved.

> It is impossible to see how segregated education is or to ignore consistently low teacher expectations, as well as apathy, sarcasm, and latent hostility present in some of the high schools. (Gersten and Keating 1987, p. 31)

A recent study by the U.S. Commission on Civil Rights (Miller 1987) claims that desegregation plans implemented over the past two decades have produced the highest level of school integration to date. This report also indicates that integration has been accompanied by massive declines in white enrollment at the same schools. And, finally, the results of bilingual language instruction appear to be equivocal, depending on which study is cited and on what the philosophical perspective of the reviewer happens to be (Mezzacappa 1987b; Crawford 1987; Gold 1987).

Evidence on the effects of early childhood programs developed during this period is also mixed. Several early examinations of Head Start have failed to find long-term positive outcomes; a recent three-year federal study corroborates those findings (Bridgman 1982). Longitudinal studies of several exemplary preschool intervention efforts that stressed cognitive development suggest more successful results: "improved intellectual performance during early childhood; better scholastic placement and improved scholastic achievement during the elementary school years; and, during adolescence, a lower rate of delinquency and higher rates of both graduation from high school and employment at age 19" (Schweinhart and Weikart 1985, p. 547). A comprehensive school-based program in New Haven that emphasizes the development of social skills as well as academic abilities at the elementary level also seems promising because it not only helps the urban youngsters involved but also develops a staff improvement model that can be replicated in other buildings (Comer, Schraft, and Sparrow 1980; Brandt 1986).

Current efforts to come to grips with the problems of educating at-risk students show we have learned much from each of the theoretical views described, as well as from the various outcomes of intervention programs pursued over the past two decades. But these efforts also indicate the problems of at-risk students have by no means been solved. High dropout rates persist. The segregation of many ethnic groups, particularly Hispanics (Report on Education Research 1987), continues to plague the social fabric of American society. Poverty, both economic and intellectual, marks the lives of many young Americans, making them victims of social as well as self-inflicted crime (Wilson 1987). What orientation do contemporary efforts take to educate at-risk students? The following three models constitute representative examples of the current scene.

Levin (1986, 1987) proposes "accelerated schools," a coordinated and comprehensive approach to educating disadvantaged students at the preschool and elementary levels. He maintains that remedial interventions are inadequate unless they substantially narrow the gap between the academic performance of disadvantaged youngsters and that of their more advantaged peers. To date, remedial efforts have generally failed to do this. Levin sees accelerated schools as transitional experiences "designed to bring disadvantaged students up to grade level by the end of sixth grade" (Levin 1987, p. 20).

Levin's accelerated approach includes four major components: providing enriched preschool experiences, improving the effectiveness of the home learning environment, improving the effectiveness of the school in addressing the needs of the disadvantaged, and assisting those from linguistically different backgrounds to acquire skills in standard English. His third component, augmenting the effectiveness of the school's resources, seems to be the most overshadowing aspect of the accelerated model because he sees the school's social-cognitive success with disadvantaged students as the antidote to the most persistent cause of dropping out: serious academic deficits. Included in Levin's view of schooling are elements of assessment used for diagnostic and program development purposes; a curriculum that emphasizes language, which is described as "reading and writing for meaning" (Levin 1987, p. 20); parental involvement in schooling; extended school days with afterschool activities in physical education and art experiences; independent assignments; and community involvement.

Levin emphasizes the importance of school-based decision making and curricular management by the teachers involved with at-risk youngsters. He is positive about the use of peer teaching and cooperative learning as significant means of "changing the organizational structure and incentives in the classroom" (Levin 1986, p. 27). Field experiments of the Levin accelerated school model opened on the West Coast in the fall of 1987; it remains to be seen if the students involved exhibit improved achievement and better self-concepts. To Levin, such "bold stands" are important and timely interventions for educators to take; he believes American society can no longer afford to neglect the needs of either at-risk students or their educators. To continue to create "educational discards" marginal to mainstream education, he suggests, is to design our own cultural demise.

Wehlage and his associates (Wehlage, Stone, and Lesko 1982; Wehlage and Rutter 1986; Wehlage, Rutter, and Turnbaugh 1987) present another current model program for working with disadvantaged secondary students, addressing, in particular, the potential problem of adolescents' dropping out of school. They believe such a program needs to be based on goals that represent some fundamental changes in the way schools interact with students and in the kinds of educational experiences they create. Although Wehlage and his colleagues are obviously aware of the critical background factors that plague at-risk students, such as poverty and minority status, they focus on what schools can actually do about the two major maladies that characterize at-risk students' schooling: boredom and alienation. At-risk learners are not challenged by their schoolwork—repetitive remediation in low-level basic skills fails to spark their interest or energy. Training in narrow vocational areas, these researchers say, suggests that the fruits of staying in school are less desirable than life on city streets, at least until the student drops out and, too late, faces the reality of being unprepared. The model program they advocate has two major goals: to provide school experiences that will engage secondary students' interest and participation, and to promote strong social bonding that leads to personal exchange with other students and with teachers.

The Wehlage model can be implemented either by using the school-within-a-school approach or by establishing an alternative site, similar to Levin's special accelerated buildings. In either case, this model advocates small, personalized settings as a departure from the factorylike, nineteenth-century units that characterize many older, large-city school systems. But the Wehlage model also addresses psychological-social space as much as physical reality. Four interrelated categories influence the model program: administration and organization, teacher culture, student culture, and curriculum. These important factors must be emphasized in creating the educational experiences at-risk youths need. Most importantly, these educators maintain that the identity and autonomy concerns faced by both the teaching staff and the students are key to student success (Wehlage, Rutter, and Turnbaugh 1987, p. 72).

The Wehlage model envisions the teacher of at-risk students as much more than a purveyor of subject matter and the school as very different from a storehouse of accumulated facts (Wehlage and Rutter 1986, p. 9). Schools are where certain commitments are made about content that is not trivial and about processes that are significant far beyond academic classrooms. Students must volunteer for this program and are required to agree to work by a common set of rules and specific standards of behavior and excellence. The model stresses individualized instruction and promotes cooperative decision making. Students work actively with close supervision by a supportive teacher. Collegiality is a goal in the overall atmosphere of the effective school. In this model, an emphasis on experiential learning, too, is often tied to real work

31

in the real world. The program must be geared to what students individually are able to do, and each student's feelings of success and accomplishment are particularly emphasized. However, only a limited part of the curriculum ought to be remedial (Wehlage and Rutter 1986).

Examination of some results following implementation of the Wehlage model has begun (Wehlage and Rutter 1986). Reducing school failure and decreasing dropout rates are the main goals of the program. Better preparing students for the world of work, as well as giving them greater feelings of self-esteem and a positive view of their control of their own existence, is an additional thrust of the model. The Wisconsin Youth Survey, an instrument developed to help assess program implementations (Wehlage and Rutter 1986, p. 15), is now being used to amass data about students' personal orientations prior to programmatic efforts and following initial treatments. Although results are not yet fully analyzed, some characteristics on the Wisconsin scale have been found to be significant in at-risk students' development. What is more important, using the survey's scale may help researchers fathom the myriad of detail about what works and what does not in such a focused effort to help at-risk students. With such an instrument, researchers may be able to identify the aspects of a strategy that are sound and those that need further development. Perhaps the most elusive characteristic, the improvement of school climate, can be more effectively dealt with on the basis of the research results from Wehlage and his associates. Given the findings of Gersten and Keating (1987) that poor educational climate still persists after some interventions, this is not a trivial accomplishment in the education of at-risk students.

Cummins (1986) of the Ontario Institute for Studies in Education has developed a third model program currently advocated to help at-risk learners. This model is particularly sensitive to difficulties of the at-risk Hispanic student, but is also applicable to minority students generally. Cummins addresses the cultural differences that exist between educational institutions and the variety of students who stand outside the majority or mainstream population. The major thrust of his approach is to alter significantly the relationships between educators and minority students and between schools and minority communities. What is required, Cummins (1986) proposes, are "personal redefinitions of the way classroom teachers interact with children and communities they serve" (p. 18). He organizes his model using three kinds of power relations that influence schooling: classroom interactions between teacher and student, relationships between schools and minority communities, and intergroup power relations within the society as a whole.

Cummins (1986) maintains the transformation he seeks is influenced by four institutional characteristics in schools that—for the sake of at-risk youngsters—need to be addressed:

- To what extent are minority students' languages and cultures incorporated into the school program?
- To what extent is minority community participation encouraged as an integral component of children's education?
- Does the pedagogy employed in school intrinsically motivate students to use language actively in order to generate their own knowledge?
- To what extent do professionals involved in assessment become advocates for minority students? (p. 21)

He proposes that previous educational reforms, which were generally ineffective in alleviating the problems of at-risk students, did not reach their goals because they ignored these issues and, thus, could not reverse the circumstances responsible for minority group failure. He sees such conflict between majority and minority populations as characteristic of the negative relationships between groups of haves and have-nots all over the world.

Obviously Cummins picks up on the multicultural or cultural pluralism theme as a viable approach for dealing with the problems of at-risk students in school at the end of the twentieth century. He is aware of demographic changes cataloged by various researchers (Hodgkinson 1985). He cites the work of Ogbu (1978, 1986) and Feuerstein (1980), among others, as discussion bases for understanding the inherent conflict between a dominant group and a dominated group in any society. Conditions of this conflict "include limited parental access to economic and educational resources, ambivalence toward cultural transmission and primary language use in the home, and interactional styles that may not prepare students for typical teacher/student interaction patterns in school" (Cummins 1986, p. 22).

Cummins then elaborates on the four issues to be faced in this context of conflict. Language needs to be "additive," he says, treating the student's bicultural-bilingual capacity as a resource for learning and stressing the meaningful power in the child's tongue as a cultural bridge to be enhanced (p. 25). He maintains that relationships encouraged between the school as an institution and the students' community will lead to positive collaboration (p. 27), and that this cooperation has a pronounced effect on students' success at school. In terms of pedagogy, Cummins stresses the need for stimulating reciprocal interaction in the classroom, encouraging student action and interdependence, and downplaying the teacher's traditional "transmission" role (p. 28). Learning requires genuine oral and written dialog between student and teacher, and this communication ideally should be integrated with curricular content that is no longer to be taught as isolated or fragmented subjects.

> In short, pedagogical approaches that empower students encourage them to assume greater control over setting their own learning goals and to collaborate actively with each other in achieving these goals. (Cummins 1986, p. 28)

Finally, in the area of assessment, Cummins sees at-risk students as largely being judged by a deficits model approach which seeks arbitrarily, on the basis of one instrument's evaluation, to label students in simplistic, unidimensional ways; evaluators have generally not attempted to then fathom out the intricacies of their learning difficulties and suggest alternate ways for drawing out their true competencies.

Experiments are needed, says Cummins, to put these four key factors into operation and to examine their effects on at-risk youngsters' performance. A few such experiments have begun, but as with Levin's and Wehlage's models, few hard data are now available to attest to the soundness of Cummins's suggested innovations. Still, he believes the knowledge necessary to propose changes in the ways schools educate at-risk students is readily available. Obviously, teachers teaching students to think need to tap into this knowledge.

TEACHING MINORITY CHILDREN

The effective instruction of minority children seems to be a key concern in addressing the cognitive development of at-risk students in American schools. Past history suggests we know some of the reasons why instruction has not been particularly effective. "A divorce between critical thinking and the basic skills helps widen the gap between schools for the poor and schools for the affluent," says Cuban (1987, p. 17); he derides the "dittos, seatwork, and pre- and post-tests" that rob at-risk students of interesting assignments which might otherwise stimulate their learning. Other researchers focus on missing interaction—or the lack of exchange—that ought to take place in the act of teaching itself. Poor teaching, observes Cummins (1986), can actually enforce negative learning on the child, and, further, he suggests minority youngsters "frequently receive intensive instruction which confines them to a passive role and induces a form of 'learned helplessness'" (p. 27). These patterns, according to Boykin (1986), are emphasized by the kind of structural sorting practiced by schools when they form remedial or retardate learning groups whose self-image is one of failure and who develop a "cannot—will not—should not do" mentality. Boykin (1986, p. 76) maintains not only that the student's cognitive orientation is involved (I cannot. . .), but also that his/her motivational state (I will not. . .) and his/her value-belief system (I should not. . .) are involved. The road to alienation and dropping out is paved with numerous small stones shaped by many classroom experiences.

The schooling of students with limited English proficiency also offers us some insight into the nature of poor instruction. Hakuta and his associates (Hakuta 1986; Hakuta and Gould 1987) propose that problems of reading need to be separated from difficulties with language. It is not the case that at-risk Spanish-speaking students cannot reason sufficiently; rather, their cognitive understanding of literacy is quite limited. Their homelives, like those of Black youngsters, are not geared to the printed word, and particular skills and instructional strategies are lacking in both English and Spanish. Laosa (1977, 1984) and De Avila and Duncan (1985) underline the socioeconomic and intellectual aspects of the Hispanic student's education. They suggest a teacher presents students with a cultural perspective as well as an academic orientation, and both aspects require two-way communication and interaction in the classroom to make learning succeed. Laosa (1979) has found more classroom teachers were prejudiced against Hispanic youngsters' language than against their divergent ethnic background. In addition, American teachers are not generally comfortable or proficient in their use of a second language (Mezzacappa 1987b).

From this extensive research and study, what seem to be the most informative guidelines for the successful instruction of minority children? Researchers on classroom instruction (Stallings 1981; Brophy and Good 1984; Brophy 1986, 1987) emphasize that good teachers stress academic objectives in setting expectations for students, and they carefully allocate instructional time. Such teachers use effective management in the classroom and pace work to keep students active and interested. They also adapt curricular materials to coordinate well with each individual student's particular learning characteristics. Brophy (1986) maintains that lower socioeconomic-status learners "need more structuring from their teachers, more active instruction and feedback, more redundancy, and small steps with high success rates" (p. 1073). This is not a departure from good instruction for all students, but Brophy agrees with Calfee (1987) that the central characteristic of good teaching is the ability to *explain* the lesson content to the learner—to explain why a strategy is useful, why certain information is important for problem resolution. At-risk youngsters may need a more extensive explanation to generate the meanings necessary for their understanding.

Many researchers today (Lipson and Wixson 1986) view interactive discussion during instruction as one of the most important aspects of effective instruction. The major concern is not one of innate skill, but under what conditions the learner employs her or his knowledge and becomes active in the learning experience. Brown and her associates (Brown 1984; Palincsar and Brown 1984; Brown, Palincsar, and Purcell 1986; Brown and Campione 1986) report on their research concerning the reciprocal teaching of comprehension-fostering activities in reading.

They conclude that at-risk youngsters have much to gain from cognitive training that includes scaffolding techniques "where an expert provides a supporting context in which students may gradually acquire skills" (Brown 1984, p. 9). They propose that seemingly disabled learners will become successful in a classroom based on such reciprocal teaching (Brown, Palincsar, and Purcell 1986). The teacher first models the desired comprehension skill; then student members in a working group gradually become jointly responsible for understanding the material and for helping their fellow students construct common meaning (Brown and Campione 1986). The importance of questioning and the role of students in self-directing and monitoring performance are stressed in this reciprocal approach (Brown, Palincsar, and Purcell 1986, p. 106), in contrast to traditional practices which may have isolated poor readers and focused on pronunciation, decoding, and relatively low-level cognitive skills. The advocates of reciprocal teaching underline the importance of learning reasoning strategies within a content domain (Brown 1984), but they are emphatic that it is the overt and explicit delineation of these specific strategies, learned collegially, that will help academically weak students deal with the particular tasks central to learning at school. They suggest, in fact, that the absence of such an approach literally creates the stereotype of a disabled learner. Parallels of the reciprocal teaching model, presented in approaches such as cooperative learning (Slavin 1980, 1981; Johnson 1981; Deutsch 1986), are also discussed extensively in the research literature. Recently, these approaches have been advocated for at-risk youngsters, too (Ascher 1986; Slavin, Karweit, and Madden 1987; Slavin 1987).

In summary, research on at-risk students' instruction suggests that a complex and growing school population is not without hope for learning in our nation's schools. Their difficulties are not trivial; demands for mastering both basic and higher-order processes in various content domains stand in sharp contrast to their underskilled and ill-motivated profiles. That schools and educators need to alter their current approaches, both in motivating and in instructing these youngsters, is evident and supported by numerous studies and various model projects. Slavin (1987) sees this thrust as a major refocusing of the entire Chapter 1 effort, the major compensatory program sponsored by the federal government. The significant question seems to be, Is our nation's educational system as a whole ready to initiate and practice what is already known in the research community?

DISCUSSION QUESTIONS

1. What are the most common characteristics of those school students called "at risk" today?

2. How are issues like dropout rates and disability concerns related to understanding who at-risk learners are in the country's schools?

3. What are three different theoretical approaches that have been used with disadvantaged students in school? Discuss the positive and negative aspects of each.

4. Describe what research suggests are the most productive ways of teaching minority children in school today.

3. THINKING SUCCESS FOR ALL STUDENTS: UNDERSTANDING THE ISSUES

by Barbara Z. Presseisen

The current interest in teaching thinking as a particular emphasis in curriculum and instruction rests on several aspects of cognitive development research carried out over the last quarter century. The importance of both cognition and metacognitive development is one of these aspects. The significance of mediation and the role of the teacher as mediator of thinking development is another. Specific programs for teaching thinking include applications of these aspects; some of these programs are herein analyzed or their research reviewed. The particular problems of at-risk learners are examined in light of what seems hopeful in teaching thinking in more direct ways. Concerns for what must be pursued to make such an innovation happen are also considered.

Proposals to make teaching thinking a focus of American education date back at least to Dewey (1910). Much of the psychological and philosophical literature of the twentieth century includes inquiries about how humans reason, critique, or judge the circumstances of their existence (Sternberg 1985b; Presseisen 1986), and Bruner (1960) launched a pedagogical movement 30 years ago to incorporate such topics into the instructional programs of elementary and secondary schools. The current movement to provide cognitive instruction to all youngsters shares these historic roots, but the present effort is based on more recent research and is responsive to a much more detailed understanding of the ways human beings recall, use, and generate information for better thinking (Chipman and Segal 1985; Jones 1986). What are the main emphases of the current movement to teach thinking to American students? What significance does such a movement have for the instruction of the country's growing at-risk population?

THE IMPORTANCE OF COGNITION AND METACOGNITION

Jones (1986) has characterized cognitive instruction "as any effort on the part of the teacher or the instructional materials to help students process information in meaningful ways and become independent learners" (p. 7). A great deal of effort has been expended in recent years to define and describe the particular skills of cognition. Thinking and learning skills, as characterized by Sternberg (1981) and cataloged in numerous studies (Beyer 1984; Costa 1985; Presseisen 1987; Marzano et al., 1988) generally include a menu of core thinking operations and various more complex, higher-order processes like problem solving, conceptualizing, decision making, critical thinking, and inventive or creative thinking. These cognitive operations are most often predictive of success at school, and many current researchers (Sternberg 1981; Chipman and Segal 1985) suggest these key behaviors constitute intelligence itself. Moreover, advocates of this movement maintain that such behaviors can be learned by all students, including those at risk (Whimbey and Whimbey 1975; Sternberg 1984).

One of the major thrusts of teaching thinking involves not only learning cognitive skills, such as analysis, classification, and evaluation, but also becoming conscious of the strategies that are appropriate in the particular cognitive task. Metacognition—thinking about how you think, or the "ability to know what we know and what we don't know" (Costa 1984, p. 57)—is now viewed as central to the development of skillful thinkers. It is not adequate to master the core thinking skills and complex processes per se; the learning-to-learn strategies that enable students to plan, monitor, and revise their own activity for more productive performance are also required for competence development and for the independence of the learner. Given the complex world students today face, Chipman and Segal (1985) suggest that the flexibility and competencies embedded in the techniques of learning *how* to learn may have the most lasting influences on student achievement.

To think metacognitively is to be concerned with the sequence of cognitive tasks. Jones (1986) reports on reading research that emphasizes what the learner does before, during, and after reading. Initially, learners should be concerned with activating prior knowledge and linking what is being learned to previously mastered materials. During the task, learners need to attend to their own activity, to monitor their comprehension as they try to complete the work. And, finally, they need to recapitulate, to review and debrief where they have been; to see what they have done both in terms of the outcomes of the work and relative to their understanding of the consequences of their performance. Sternberg (1983) sees a similar sequence in the learner's building of executive skills in general problem solving. He proposes a nine-step pattern including identifying the problem; selecting processes, strategies, and representation; allocating resources; monitoring solutions; dealing with feedback; and, finally, translating activity into action planning and then into problem resolution. In intellectual development, metacognition lies at the heart of Sternberg's executive component.

39

The literature on metacognition also stresses the importance of independent thinking. The learner's disposition toward being a critical thinker needs to be fostered as she or he learns to be metacognitive. Ennis's (1985) research on critical thinking over the past 30 years highlights such characteristics. Learners who are flexible and open-minded, who seek alternatives, and who persist in carrying out a task will be more effective. Costa (1985) stresses the significance of students' being able to talk freely about potential problem solutions with their peers and of their having the opportunity in the classroom to develop new strategies and to practice them on their own. While many theorists emphasize the direct teaching of the more basic cognitive skills, it may be that we cannot teach metacognition directly. However, some say freely experiencing metacognitive realizations is key to acquiring the higher-order thinking abilities. Kamii (1984) underlines the importance of giving each learner autonomy, which includes the freedom to err and the right to be respected even when making mistakes.

Researchers stress that metacognitive ability is something that grows and develops over time. One experience with the scientific method or an odd lesson or two that emphasize problem solving or information generation will probably not be sufficient to develop metacognition. What particularly counts is the development of an open attitude toward thinking, reasoning, and dealing with data. Nickerson (1986b) notes the parallels between reasoning and the task of figuring out what to believe; the thinker must first gather all the evidence relative to an issue, then weigh the evidence as impartially as possible, and finally decide what explanation is the best or most fitting. Better thinkers develop "nuanced judgment," says Resnick (1985), after they have experience with content and after they wrangle extensively with problems rooted in contextual relationships. Although thinking skills can be learned in content-incidental and perhaps even content-free situations, most advocates of cognitive instruction (Glaser 1984; Kuhn 1986) stress the importance of mastering skills embedded in specific subject disciplines. The methods of the particular discipline reflect the rules or criteria of problem solving in that domain, and such standards are not unrelated to the appropriate strategies one builds over time in developing metacognitive ability.

THE ROLE OF MEDIATION IN THE CLASSROOM

A second major thrust in the movement to teach thinking focuses on the role of the teacher as a mediator of learning in the classroom. Not only is the teacher important because of the need to instruct students directly in the core thinking skills, and perhaps in the complex or higher-order processes, but also it is proposed that the teacher's influence on students' cognitive processing of the lessons themselves is highly significant. How the learning is managed, how interactive exchange occurs in the classroom, and how students get feedback to their responses all influence the quality of mediation in instruction (Costa 1984).

The teacher's role as a questioner and a respondent to questions is one of the most discussed aspects of classroom mediation. Wassermann (1987) suggests some teacher responses can inhibit or even stop a student's thoughtful pursuit of an issue. Teachers can ask questions that are so low level, they fail to engage students' thinking and, all too often, teach that learning consists of simple, one-word answers to queries seemingly unattached to other issues or to more complex sources of information. Ideally, teacher questioning in the thinking classroom should turn students back onto their own ideas, raise the matter being considered to higher levels of cognitive reflection, and suggest different and challenging ways of looking at the same problem. Haywood (1986) suggests a series of questions and requests that teachers might use to enhance classroom mediation:

1. What do you need to do next?
2. Tell me how you did that.
3. What do you think would happen if _____?
4. When have you done something like this before?
5. How would you feel if _____?
6. Yes, that's right, but how did you know it was right?
7. When is another time you need to _____?
8. What do you think the problem is?
9. Can you think of another way we could do this?
10. Why is this one better than that one?
11. How can you find out?
12. How is _____ different (like) _____? (p. 3)

It is interesting to note how many of these questions urge students indirectly to the next best metacognitive consideration.

Copple, Sigel, and Saunders (1984) caution educators not to interfere with questions when young learners are busy doing their work; the wise teacher waits for appropriate times to intervene. Similarly, they suggest that teachers shouldn't steal a student's thunder by answering a question before they have given the student adequate time to reply. The research on wait time in classroom activity confirms such a mediational stance. The teacher's social and affective support of the student is also an important aspect of mediation in the thinking classroom. Although the teacher is the prime interrogator during initial learning, good teaching of thinking occurs in a social setting, and students need to be brought into the interaction positively and be willing to be engaged.

Much of the current research on teaching thinking reflects a renewed interest in the work of Vygotsky, a Russian neuropsychologist, and in the studies of Feuerstein, an Israeli clinical psychologist, both of whom stress the importance of the learner's experience as influenced by linguistic exchange and by the intervention of the classroom teacher.

Much of what the teacher says, believes, and does in a classroom influences students' perceptions of their own abilities, their personal view of themselves and their own competence, and their motivation to pursue the cognitive tasks at hand. Feuerstein (1981) stresses the importance of classroom communication patterns. Through communicating in a variety of ways, he says, the teacher conveys three important aspects of mediation: intentionality, anticipation, and meaning. Intentionality engages the learner in perceiving, registering, or performing; anticipation takes the student beyond the immediate, to learn to deal with the consequences of thought and action in the future; and meaning gets at the heart of understanding and comprehension (Feuerstein 1981, p. 97). Vygotsky (1962) speaks of the child's "zone of proximal development," the potential that every child possesses for learning based on personal experience, but that is separate from development itself. By carefully observing what every learner does, the teacher builds an index of those developmental functions students are in the process of completing (Portes 1985). The teacher then can become aware of each student's unique mental profile and anticipate what the overall needs of the entire class of youngsters will be in learning particular content or subject matter.

Finally, mediation suggests that learners only gradually develop their own self-regulative behavior—that is, some learners do. Kuhn (1986) suggests we need to take a life-span approach to understanding changes in the child's thinking. As they gain experience in solving problems, as they begin to see patterns of strategies that are useful for working in particular content domains, better thinkers correct their "theories" and "mini-theories" and revise their interpretations of classroom work. From her constructivist view, Kuhn sees "cognitive development as a process of theory revision" (p. 508). In the long run, learning to think for all students is learning to self-correct or regulate, and the teacher's mediational role ought to contribute directly to that progression. Work by Resnick (1985) and Glaser (1984) on the development of expert systems suggests a similar position regarding learning and cognitive development.

We ought to consider, too, the role of assessment and testing in the self-regulatory development of thinkers. Potentially, tests show what students don't know, as well as what they seemingly understand. As a result, we must raise serious concerns regarding the kinds of evaluative instruments used to analyze students' cognitive performance. In the teaching of thinking, tests ideally ought to get to the basic understandings behind content comprehension. Jones (1986) rejects norm-referenced tests as measures of individual achievement because they fail to attend to the student's cognitive development and because they often stress only low-level thinking objectives. Rather, she suggests, we should employ content-referenced examinations in the teaching of thinking. Such instruments can evaluate what actually has been taught and understood, as well as better inform the teacher about what is still needed in classroom instruction. Obviously, testing as a mediational tool for learning requires that the assessments both serve the students' cognitive needs and inform the teacher's classroom practices. This requirement may be even more important for underachieving learners, partly because they require more diagnosis and partly because they are harmed more by low-level tests.

MATERIALS AND PROGRAMS FOR TEACHING THINKING

A third notable activity in the current movement to teach thinking is the development of instructional materials and programs to use in elementary, secondary, and even college classrooms. Unfortunately, finding or using such specific materials is often the practitioner's first step, even before he or she has understood or examined the major conceptual understandings of teaching thinking (Sternberg 1987; Presseisen 1987). In this chapter we cannot begin to describe or analyze the wealth of thinking materials which has recently been produced, but discussion of the general nature of major programs and their potential use with at-risk students is warranted.

Thinking-skills programs differ on many dimensions, as Nickerson (1984) has indicated, but all of them generally emphasize some specific cognitive operations which are delineated in the materials provided to a particular group of students. Thus, some programs emphasize a variety of skills—such as general reasoning, learning-to-learn skills, and problem solving. Other programs stress critical thinking above other concerns, and still others advocate teaching creativity and expanding intellectual processing in a variety of modes or with specific kinds of materials. Costa (1985) has described a number of curricular programs in his useful volume *Developing Minds*, and readers can check there for developer descriptions of such programs as *Strategic Reasoning*, *Odyssey*, and *Structure of Intellect* which emphasize a variety of thinking skills; *Philosophy for Children* and *Project Impact* which stress critical thinking; and *CoRT* and *Instrumental Enrichment* which emphasize the development of expansive mental processes and divergent thinking heuristics. These programs are very representative of the large variety of curricular approaches available to teach thinking.

43

Most thinking programs are based on a particular conceptual focus and take some position on the need for special teacher preparation to use the material. The developers of *Philosophy for Children* and *Instrumental Enrichment*, for example, require relatively extensive teacher preparation to instruct their programs. They have particular ideas about how skills are developed, what student behaviors are being sought, and how learning ought to be assessed (Lipman, Sharp, and Oscanyan 1980; Feuerstein et al. 1985; Link 1985). Other developers focus less on the teacher's involvement and more on the students' motivation to use their own cognitive abilities. *CoRT* requires a minimum of teacher preparation, but its developer seeks to involve students in new ways of looking at problems and imaginative schemes for resolving them (de Bono 1967, 1985). The developers of *Tactics*, originally the McREL Thinking Skills program (Marzano and Hutchins 1985), take somewhat of a middle ground between the need for preparing teachers and the need for generating interesting examples of activities to show teachers how to embed important cognitive tasks into the content they are teaching. Some programs are not really curricular entities at all, but rather are approaches or strategies for relating the teaching of thinking to regular classroom activity and curricula, as well as to general planning for instruction and assessment (Worsham and Stockton 1985; Meyers 1986; Beyer 1987).

This wealth of material indicates there is no ideal thinking-skills program; in fact, there are many approaches. These approaches differ according to the intentions of the author or developer, and in terms of what is considered the most important aspect of learning to think. Nearly every approach addresses the cognitive and metacognitive skills of learning. To various degrees, programs delineate the kinds of mediational behavior expected of the teacher, and, to a lesser extent, the role of assessment or testing is generally discussed. Programs differ, too, with regard to the populations for which they are intended, including the age group, the particular needs of students, and their conditions of learning. The user must match the needs of his/her student population to the appropriate instructional materials for teaching them to think. It may be that no commercially available program will serve a particular schooling situation. However, before they reach this conclusion, users need to develop criteria for making a program selection or plan, and let these standards serve as guidelines for their deliberations. Some researchers (Nickerson 1984; Sternberg 1985a) have considered the contents of such criteria; central to many of their considerations is the question of a particular program's effectiveness.

Ideally, we should have clear, clean data on the various thinking-skills programs and their ability to accomplish what they have set out to achieve. Unfortunately, such unequivocal proof does not exist. Many of the programs for teaching thinking have concentrated their energies on developing materials and guidelines for instructors; few have had the resources to run extensive, long-term research projects to determine the outcomes of implementation. However, this is not to say the research has not been conducted or that studies of implementations of particular programs are not available.

Sternberg (1986) has reviewed the research on five well-known, diverse programs: *Instrumental Enrichment, Philosophy for Children, Structure of Intellect, Problem Solving and Comprehension*, and *Odyssey*. He found the studies of these programs contained many contaminating factors and lacked consistent research data. But he also found hopeful signs and called for more formal research on program implementations by objective, independent, and skilled researchers. Savell, Twohig, and Rachford (1986) have conducted extensive studies of Feuerstein's *Instrumental Enrichment* (FIE) program, and although they conclude that worldwide efforts "failed to find clear FIE effects," they also note that "there is a subset that produced data that are striking and suggest that FIE may indeed be having an effect even though it is not clear just what that effect means" (p. 401). They found that statistically significant FIE/comparison group differences have been observed in a number of populations in at least four different countries. The outcomes most often reported in these studies have included effects on certain standard nonverbal means of intelligence, largely measures of skill in processing figural and spatial information. These same researchers have determined 12- to 18-year-olds seem to be most influenced by the FIE program. Sternberg (1986) reports similar findings on the Feuerstein program.

Herrnstein et al. (1986) have reported on studies of *Project Intelligence*, the forerunner of the *Odyssey* program that was implemented in Venezuela in a Spanish language edition. They conclude "a 56-lesson course directed toward fundamental cognitive skills was shown to have sizable and beneficial effects on a sample of Venezuelan seventh graders from economically and educationally deprived backgrounds" (p. 1288). They particularly note that a new, dynamic interaction between teacher and students resulted from the program, and suggest that the course profoundly changed the classroom for both teacher and students.

The *Philosophy for Children* program recently released an extensive review of fourteen research studies conducted at numerous sites across the United States over the past fifteen years (Institute for the Advancement of Philosophy for Children 1986). The report shows the program achieved impressive results in accomplishing its goals with a variety of school populations, including urban Black and Hispanic groups. Most of these studies used the New Jersey Test of Basic Skills as their major assessment instrument. Individual school districts reporting on a one- or

45

two-year implementation of the philosophy program may not yet have found significant score changes for students in mathematics or reading, as reported by standardized examinations, but some districts have attributed to the program decided improvement in students' abilities to reason and to discuss complex issues, including drug and alcohol abuse, as well as improved teacher performance (Shipman 1982; Martin and Weinstein 1984). These findings suggest how important it is that we understand what objectives a thinking program proposes and follow the ways such objectives are pursued in the material.

Research on *Project Impact*, a National Diffusion Network bona fide program, suggests the critical thinking orientation of the program does relate well to language arts and social studies instruction in the middle school (Zinner 1985). Mathematics teachers have also suggested this critical thinking approach helped underachieving students better understand the nature of mathematics problems, while other instructors have claimed teacher morale improved with use of the program. *Project Impact* has also had success in a Spanish language version.

Research on the *CoRT* thinking materials, although not as extensive as studies of the Feuerstein approach or of *Philosophy for Children*, has suggested the de Bono approach has a positive influence on some delinquent and violent youngsters in England, as well as validity as an approach for analytic discourse in an Australian science classroom (de Bono 1985). Edwards and Baldauf (1987) report *CoRT-1* significantly helped students on their normal teacher-designed, content-based academic tests—especially in language arts and social science courses.

In sum, impressive but not conclusive data have been amassed on the effectiveness of numerous thinking-skills programs and materials with a variety of students and in a variety of school settings. de Bono (1985) makes a distinction between hard data and soft results. The research evidence to date does not provide clear, significant, quantitative information based on "a large number of implementations, specific factors, and replicable systematic conditions," as called for by Sternberg and Bhana (1986, p. 67). Rather, some of the larger, more global objectives of the thinking programs indicate positive changes in the general nature of many students regarding intelligent behavior.

> . . .the confidence of those who have had training in thinking, the focus of their thinking, the effectiveness of their thinking, their structured approach and breadth of consideration. Teachers often sum up these factors as "maturity," in commenting about these children who come to their classrooms after some training in thinking. (de Bono 1985, p. 208)

Perhaps some real opportunities for major, quantifiable change lie behind such "soft" results; obviously, more research and more implementation are needed to pursue these possibilities. What is important, suggests Nickerson (1986a), is that children be given the chance through regular instruction to practice thinking and to model the examples their teachers provide in motivating, cognitive instructional lessons. What is also significant, it would seem, is that at-risk students must be given just as much opportunity to experience this type of instruction as their more able peers.

THINKING, ACHIEVEMENT, AND AT-RISK STUDENTS

Can the teaching of thinking help educators better understand the problems they face in addressing the challenge of improving the education of at-risk students? Can the experience of the cognitive instruction movement inform the nation's educators in working with the growing population of young people who fail to find success in academic work at school? There is much to interrelate between the two major areas of investigation reviewed in the above discussions. In the end, several overarching issues emerge as key concerns.

First, many American educators seem to doubt whether at-risk students *can* learn to be successful learners. Levin's (1986, 1987) and Wehlage's (Wehlage and Rutter 1986) special accelerated approaches may be efforts in the right direction, but they need to be made available to all at-risk students, and they need to address the question of how to concentrate on some particular skills, at special times of development, and related in specific ways to the content domains of regular schooling. At the heart of the issue is what kinds of achievement we expect at-risk youngsters to attain. Reform programs that set out to show gains mainly in terms of standardized test results may have limited success, as the results from many of the thinking-skills programs have indicated. Educators may need to explore the differences between hard and soft data on student change, as de Bono suggests. Further, we may need to define *remedial* learning more fully. Shouldn't we address the *potential* for learning in underachieving youngsters, as Feuerstein (1979) proposes, rather than merely looking at their deficits? Feuerstein presents his Learning Potential Assessment Device as such an innovative instrument to obtain better diagnostic data on youngsters with difficulties. Educators who implement programs for at-risk learners may need to consider that their charges are only *temporarily* disabled and that better teaching conditions can contribute to the advancement of these youngsters. Children *are* modifiable in terms of their intelligent behavior; starting early in their development, as recommended by advocates of the Perry Preschool model (Berrueta-Clement et al. 1984), may be an important maneuver to avoid students' dropping out after grade nine. But equally important in that effort are the kinds of skills that comprise the overarching goals of such a program.

47

Second, the emphasis on higher-order thinking and not on "just basic skills" is a key concern in addressing the education of at-risk students. Keeping lesser-achieving students only in the realm of the basic may mean they will be dependent thinkers all their lives. Given the experience of the thinking-skills programs, teaching metacognitive behavior may be one of the most important goals to pursue in the education of at-risk students. These students are episodic in their learning, they fail to make connections that others may see more spontaneously, and too often they miss the central meaning that is key to learning. Thinking-skills programs and related materials have addressed these areas, both in curricular ways and through alternative instruction. Educators of at-risk students should be mindful of the emphasis on metacognition in teaching thinking and learn about the successes that certain programs have had in meeting that objective.

A third and very significant aspect that we may focus on in teaching thinking successfully to at-risk students is the unique role of the teacher in classroom instruction. As Wehlage and his associates (Wehlage and Rutter 1986) emphasize, social bonding—the mediational role of the teacher—needs to be expanded in the education of at-risk learners. What unique mix of classroom coach, gentle questioner, high motivator, and steady guide do we need to achieve to work in the thoughtful classroom of new-found learners? This is an area of concern for pre-service as much as in-service educators, for teacher education as well as staff development. The use of language in instruction is significant to the role of the effective teacher of at-risk learners. Boyer (1987) has stressed the centrality of language in education; the research on teaching thinking underlines the importance of language not only as the form of presentation—reading—but also as the lifeblood of communication. Teaching at-risk youngsters to think and to express their ideas about the meaningfulness of content domains provides an area for extensive dialog between the teachers of critical thinking and the instructors of middle and secondary school classrooms. It is not only a matter of reading, for there are many literacies to teach (Eisner 1987). We need to treat these cognitive areas differently, and we need to be as concerned with remediating the cognitive processes of at-risk students as we are with building new meaning in learning contents. As Cummins (1986) proposes, studying the ways language bridges the gap between not understanding and knowing is a major challenge for the mediational education of at-risk youngsters. When language is related to cognitive learning and development, and the at-risk students in question also happen to speak Spanish as their mother tongue, we may need to consider different and varied issues.

And, finally, the aspect of policy development seems to emerge as a major concern when we consider teaching at-risk students through the lens of cognitive instruction. Are there practices or policies that we really need to reexamine as supportive or destructive of at-risk students' development? What significance might grouping practices have for teaching at-risk students with a cognitive emphasis? What guidelines for maximizing resources, both human and physical, do we need to develop? How important is it that we pursue positive school and classroom environments that encourage collegial contact for both students and teachers? What role does the district staff or the building principal play in giving the classroom teacher control over the major decisions on sound and thoughtful instruction? The current thinking-skills movement is no advocate of teacher-proof curricula or mandated learning programs untouched by the instructors' decision making. Many personnel policy issues addressed by the current approaches for dealing with at-risk students are also addressed by the innovative thinking programs.

Ultimately, good teaching and high regard are the greatest potential bonuses for the at-risk student, just as they are for the gifted or regular student. We need to take care to be aware of the particular insufficiencies of the at-risk student because he/she is only a novice at thinking and needs to be aided in gaining insight into his or her own better thought and performance. For too long, perhaps, educators have neglected to encourage the connections of student thought processes with the more complex structures of thinking. In the end, the greatest educational danger our society faces by not addressing the cognitive needs of this special population is that at-risk students will be ill-served by never knowing what they don't know. Further, they will have missed opportunities to acquire the higher-level skills that could make them capable of transforming their own lives. At the current juncture of circumstances in American education, we have a unique chance to deal effectively with the regular schooling of at-risk students in our population. What does this opportunity for educational reform imply for the work that lies ahead of us?

IMPLICATIONS FOR THE FUTURE

If we accept the notion that teaching thinking to at-risk students is a beneficial goal for both students and American education, how should we pursue such an effort and what concerns do we need to monitor? Many of the implications for the future are related to the issues previously discussed.

The Need for Teacher Advocates

Teaching thinking to at-risk students requires instructors who are positive and caring about youngsters and who, in fact, believe such students are both malleable and modifiable. At the same time, the teaching of cognitive development necessitates professional personnel who are knowledgeable in a number of ways. They must be familiar with thinking-skills materials and cognizant of the literature and research on thinking and problem solving. They must be conversant, too, in the active instruction of, about, and for thinking, and aware of ways to use each approach to teaching thinking to at-risk students.

Teachers who seek to deal effectively with at-risk students need to work simultaneously on several dimensions of the classroom environment. Mediation and motivation are essential concerns, even before cognitive tasks are attacked in depth. Teachers need to view the "classroom as a social group for figuring out best answers," says Brown (1984, p. 18). They must consider the individual needs of at-risk students, as well as the characteristics of an entire class. Such instructors should want to collaborate with their peers in selecting the best practices for teaching at-risk children and be open to including the children's families in some of the learning activities.

Teachers who advocate helping at-risk students improve their thinking ability should be able to focus on meaningful connections that help explain to youngsters why certain relationships are logical and real. "Teaching becomes a delicate balance among content goals, strategies required for achieving those goals, and the experiences students bring to their learning," says Knoll (1987, p. vii) in introducing the concept of strategic teaching developed by Jones and her associates. At the same time, effective teachers must forge in their own minds the relationships between classroom activity and the content disciplines they teach, as well as understandings of the real world in which minority children live. The contexts of learning for at-risk children are complex and potentially unfamiliar to the college-educated instructor. Such contexts are certainly not easily captured in textbook depictions of urban education.

Finally, teacher advocates must be sensitive to the expression and language they use to relate to at-risk learners. Body language, oral speech, expectations, responses, and praise all enter into the intricate and diplomatic exchanges of value in a classroom. If alienation and boredom are the heritage of past experiences in teaching at-risk students, teachers must be ready to counter such foes both individually and collectively.

The Need for Long-Term Change

Teaching thinking to at-risk students is neither a quick fix activity nor simply a recipe-based sequence of canned programming. Personalized knowledge and self-regulated monitoring grow slowly in learners and need to be tied to real experiences and meaningful detail. Programs that emphasize continuous progress, made at a student's individual pace, have been most successful with at-risk students, and good thinking efforts should probably be no different (Slavin 1987).

Starting cognitive education with young children seems to offer the possibility of having an impact that can be sustained. Obviously, we stand a better chance of preventing students from dropping out if our efforts begin in preschool settings rather than in the middle grades or during the adolescent years. This does not preclude work in the middle grades or during adolescence, for much research suggests these are still formative times for development. However, providing a variety of experiences in the early years and changing work groups frequently, rather than locking youngsters into convenient, restrictive categories, ought to be regular practices that will encourage long-term student gains.

Teachers of cognitive instruction need to focus on ways to develop student autonomy over time, to help at-risk youngsters learn to take control of their own learning wherever that occurs. For students living in America's urban ghettos, realizing the importance of their own responsibility for learning is one of the most essential aspects of learning. It is the mark of maturity as an individual and the challenge to be a full-fledged member of a democratic society. Higher-order skills must be made applicable on the city streets as well as in the classroom. At least in the classroom they can be teacher-nurtured.

The Need for a Better Integrated Curriculum, K–12

A focus on thinking-based education for all students, including those at risk of academic failure, highlights the need for integrating cognitive instruction into the regular curriculum of the school. The subject matter ideas need to be interrelated with the student's skills and processes in productive thinking, and the learner's strategies of metacognition and problem solving need to be allied with the methodologies of various school subjects. Students as well as teachers need to make these curricular connections.

We should not view such an integration of cognition and curriculum as a response to a simplistic war between content and process. Contrary to some scholars' views of the cognitive approach to instruction (Cheyney 1987), teaching thinking is neither devoid of content nor necessarily removed from the concerns of subject matter knowledge. Nor is teaching thinking simply the provision of techniques for recalling important facts or unconnected trivia. Such views miss a great deal of what cognitive instruction is all about; in particular, such approaches miss what is the teacher's major challenge in working with at-risk learners. Teaching history, or geometry, or literature to students who

51

live in an urban housing project requires the teacher to know the subject matter content in terms of potential ideas for the classroom. But it also requires the teacher to be mindful of how content can be made meaningful to those particular students, within the context of real classroom dynamics, and relative to the chemistry of interaction among the students themselves.

Shulman (1986, 1987) emphasizes that of the various forms of knowledge a teacher must address in promoting comprehension among students, pedagogical content knowledge—knowing how to relate ideas of the academic subject matter to the teachable situation—is the professional educator's unique domain. Being a successful teacher, which he likens to being a symphony conductor (Shulman 1987, p. 2), means helping students see a content area develop through multiple levels of meaning (simple translation, relationships, interpretation, application, and evaluation) until the ideas become their own. Shulman describes an ideal English teacher as one who strives to liberate her secondary students' minds through literacy. She wants them to use the contents of the literature curriculum at school ultimately to illuminate their own lives. If she were working with at-risk youngsters, she would need to see that earlier levels of meaning have been mastered first. She also would need to interest students in the work initially and to challenge their involvement in and intrinsic motivation for the learning itself.

Content areas of the school's program are only beginning to address the cognitive challenge for improved instruction. Reading and writing specialists have begun to consider the issues of thinking in developing programs and courses for student comprehension and understanding (Jones et al. 1987; Harris and Cooper 1985). Mathematicians, scientists, and instructors of various arts are addressing problem solving and creative involvement issues with student thinking in mind (Dillon and Sternberg 1986). Some practitioners are concentrating their efforts on at-risk students' difficulties (Orr 1987), but schools have a long way to go to make the ideal real. In many classrooms, teachers still present content as an accumulation of facts unrelated to ideas within the teaching discipline itself, let alone correlated to other areas of knowledge. Many textbooks and instructional materials serve the goal of coverage in a content area, but fail to be concerned with a student's developing awareness of a discipline or with the ways she or he builds up strategies for resolving problems in particular contexts. Successful thinking-skills programs can be sources of information and examples for developing cognitive-based curricula. Classroom teachers, in particular, can benefit from knowledge of programs like *Philosophy for Children*, *CoRT*, and *Instrumental Enrichment*—and especially from the implementation of these programs with at-risk youngsters.

The Need to Develop District and Building Support

For any innovation to take hold in an educational environment and certainly to continue and thrive in real classrooms and buildings, the leadership of the particular institutions involved needs to be knowledgeable and supportive of the change. To succeed, teaching thinking to at-risk youngsters has to become a significant goal for district leadership and building principals. As the thrust of a major program effort, teaching thinking has to be integrated into the regular sequence of decision making regarding curriculum, instruction, and assessment in the given organization.

Three particular factors seem to influence the quality of support that a district might give to a thinking program initiative. Allocating time for teachers and district leaders to meet, plan, and discuss their program is essential. Regularly scheduled project time can be a vital ingredient in an effective program. Determining human and material resources is another significant aspect of program support. Quantity of funds need not dominate a project; but lack of funding shows it is not valued. And, thirdly, coordinating staff development work with the need to develop a thinking-skills effort can give a major boost to a cognitive instructional initiative. Given the understanding of how important the teaching staff's control of decision making is to program success, leadership needs to focus on enabling staff to take charge of the project, not on directing them on the administration's preferences for project management. Reform by remote control, says Cuban (1987), doesn't work at state levels or within large districts.

In order for a thinking-oriented project to be launched successfully and effect long-term change, the community surrounding the school, and especially the families of students themselves, needs to be aware and supportive of the cognitive approach. Thinking and intellectual development need to be valued in the larger community, and tie-ins to employment possibilities and community agencies are important adjuncts for a program that seeks to influence the lives of at-risk students. We must bridge the gap between the world of urban students and that of more advantaged learners as we pave the way for higher education or advanced training. Several efforts to make these connections are under way in large districts (Montague 1987; Mezzacappa 1987c); they merit watching for future outcomes.

The Need to Examine Current Policies and Practices

Finally, launching a thinking-skills project for at-risk students may require a district or a school to reexamine its prior policies and practices in light of the goals of cognitive instruction. Grouping and tracking policies, promotion standards, testing and assessment practices, curriculum planning and development, and teacher evaluation might all be addressed differently if the major desired program outcomes include teaching students to think critically and to be independent learners. These policies and practices need to be debated and deliberated by the professional staff who will conduct the project. Such debate and deliberation are extensive learning mechanisms. In the long run, discussion about such issues will educate a staff on the deeper meaning of cognitive instruction for their school community.

In conclusion, this and the preceding chapter have examined two large literatures—one on at-risk students and the other on cognitive instruction or teaching thinking—and have considered whether their interrelationship seems to provide the basis for a wise and productive initiative for the future of American education. That there are obvious relationships and hopeful areas of collaboration seems well documented here. Perhaps even more than other students in our schools, at-risk learners need to be able to figure things out and to be independent learners. That is an important aspect of equity in American schooling.

But this examination also shows that learning to think autonomously requires practice and gradual progress in a number of cognitive and metacognitive skills. The influence of the teacher is key to the learning, and teachers of thinking need to be knowledgeable about their subject matter, their students and their abilities, and the teachable situations around which schooling is organized. This has significant implications for both teacher education and continuous staff development. Moreover, cognitive learning depends a great deal on the motivation of both the student and the teacher—we are all "proximal" and derive meaning from that which is closest to us. As Bransford and his associates (Bransford et al. 1987) suggest, cognitive learning needs to be "anchored" in instruction that is parallel to personal interests and contexts.

Many questions are raised by the association of teaching thinking and at-risk students, and we obviously need further research to answer some of them. How exactly do at-risk youngsters learn best? What influence do the new instructional materials on thinking skills have on student achievement after several years of implementation? How can content domains best be integrated with thinking strategies so at-risk students will appreciate them? These research areas need to be pursued, even while cognitive instruction is begun in the classroom.

At least this topic gives educational reformers much food for thought about the burgeoning at-risk population filling America's classrooms. We cannot simply tell these at-risk students what's to be done. They need to understand it in terms of the serious nature of the intellectual crisis in which they live. A vignette from a north Philadelphia neighborhood serves to illustrate this point. The mayor's Anti-Graffiti Network recently painted a wall of a city housing project in collaboration with the local community. "Say No To Drugs," says the wall mural, "And Our Children Will Be Saved." The youngsters of that project need to realize that the directive about drugs is a critical-thinking and decision-making challenge, not a mere command. The marketing of illegal drugs puts every person in that neighborhood at risk of survival, and only by realizing what an individual can do to fight the helplessness of such victimization can the community hope to overcome such situations. Thinking for every child in American society may be the first step in retrieving the birthright of a democratic republic. In that north Philadelphia neighborhood, saying no to drugs as a conscious, self-monitoring, and autonomous act can return the metaphor to its religious roots. It is the children of America who will be saved—*Sybil* and *Pygmalion* notwithstanding.

DISCUSSION QUESTIONS

1. What is metacognition, and how is it related to a student's developing cognitive ability?

2. To be a good mediator in the classroom, what are some alternate ways in which a teacher can question students during instruction?

3. If teachers are looking for commercially packaged thinking programs for at-risk students, what factors should they consider about each program?

4. If hard data results cannot be cited with regard to using thinking-skills programs with at-risk students, why should teachers of these students become familiar with such programs?

REFERENCES

Anrig, G. R. 1985. Educational standards, testing, and equity. *Phi Delta Kappan* 66(9): 623–26.

Ansara, A.; Geshwind, N.; Galaburda, A.; Albert, M.; and Gartrell, N., eds. 1981. *Sex differences in dyslexia*. Towson, Md.: Orton Dyslexia Society.

Ascher, C. 1986. Cooperative learning in the urban classroom. *ERIC/CUE Digest* 30: 1–4.

Ascher, C. 1987. The ninth grade—A precarious time for the potential dropout. *ERIC/CUE Digest* 34:1–4.

Banks, J. A. 1982. Educating minority youths: An inventory of current theory. *Education and Urban Society* 15(1): 88–103.

Belmont, J. M; Butterfield, E. C.; and Ferretti, R. P. 1982. To secure transfer of training: Instruct self-management skills. In *How and how much can intelligence be increased,* ed. D. K. Detterman and R. J. Sternberg, 147–54. Norwood, N.J.: Ablex.

Bereiter, C., and Englemann, S. 1966. *Teaching disadvantaged children in the preschool.* Englewood Cliffs, N.J.: Prentice-Hall.

Berrueta-Clement, J. R.; Schweinhart, L. J.; Barnett, W. S.; Epstein, A. S.; and Weikart, D. P. 1984. *Changed lives: The effects of the Perry Preschool Program on youths through age 19.* Ypsilanti, Mich.: The High/Scope Press.

Beyer, B. K. 1984. Improving thinking skills—Defining the problem. *Phi Delta Kappan* 65(7): 486–90.

Beyer, B. K. 1987. *Practical strategies for the teaching of thinking.* Boston: Allyn & Bacon.

Bloom, B.; Davis, A.; and Hess, R. 1965. *Compensatory education for cultural deprivation.* New York: Holt, Rinehart & Winston.

de Bono, E. 1967. *New think: The use of lateral thinking in the generation of new ideas.* New York: Basic Books.

de Bono, E. 1985. The CoRT thinking program. In *Developing minds: A resource book for teaching thinking,* ed. A. L. Costa, 203–209. Alexandria, Va.: Association for Supervision and Curriculum Development.

Boyer, E. L. 1987. Early schooling and the nation's future. *Educational Leadership* 44(6): 4–6.

Boykin, A. W. 1986. The triple quandary and the schooling of Afro-American children. In *The school achievement of minority children: New perspectives,* ed. U. Neisser, 57–92. Hillsdale, N. J.: Lawrence Erlbaum Associates.

Brandt, R. S. 1986. On improving achievement of minority children: A conversation with James Comer. *Educational Leadership* 43(5): 13–17.

Bransford, J. D.; Burns, M. S.; Delclos, V. R.; and Vye, N. J. 1986. Teaching thinking: Evaluating evaluations and broadening the data base. *Educational Leadership* 44(2): 68–70.

Bransford, J. D.; Sherwood, R. D.; Hasselbring, T. S.; Kinzer, C. K.; and Williams, S. M. 1987. *Anchored instruction: Why we need it and how technology can help.* Nashville: Vanderbilt University, George Peabody College for Teachers. Photocopy.

Bridgman, A. 1982. Head Start's benefits are short-lived, a three-year federal study concludes. *Education Week* 5(2): 1, 15.

Brophy, J. 1986. Teacher influences on student achievement. *American Psychologist* 41(10): 1069–77.

Brophy, J. 1987. *Research linking teacher behavior to student achievement: Potential implications for instruction of Chapter 1 students.* East Lansing, Mich.: Institute for Research on Teaching. Photocopy.

Brophy, J., and Good, T. L. 1984. *Teacher behavior and student achievement.* Occasional Paper no. 73. East Lansing, Mich.: Institute for Research on Teaching.

Brown, A. L. 1984. Teaching students to think as they read: Implications for curriculum reform. Paper presented for the American Educational Research Association Project:

Research Contributions for Educational Improvement. Washington, D.C.: American Educational Research Association.

Brown, A. L., and Campione, J. C. 1986. Psychological theory and the study of learning disabilities. *American Psychologist* 14(10): 1059–68.

Brown, A. L.; Palincsar, A. S.; and Purcell, L. 1986. Poor readers: Teach, don't label. In *The school achievement of minority children: New perspectives*, ed. U. Neisser, 105–43. Hillsdale, N.J.: Lawrence Erlbaum Associates.

Bruner, J. S. 1960. *The process of education*. New York: Vintage Books.

Calfee, R. C. 1987. Those who can explain, teach. . . . *Educational Policy* 1(1): 9–27.

Cardenas, J. A. 1986. The role of native-language instruction in bilingual education. *Phi Delta Kappan* 67(5): 359–63.

Cheyney, L. V. 1987. *American memory: A report on the humanities in the nation's public schools*. Washington, D.C.: National Endowment for the Humanities.

Chipman, S. F., and Segal, J. W. 1985. Higher cognitive goals for education: An introduction. In *Thinking and learning skills*. Vol. 2, *Research and open questions*, ed. S. F. Chipman, J. W. Segal, and R. Glaser, 1–18. Hillsdale, N.J.: Lawrence Erlbaum Associates.

Church, G. J. 1985. Hispanics: A melding of cultures. *Time*, 8 July, 34–39.

Cohen, E. G., and De Avila, E. 1983. *Learning to think in math and science: Improving local education for minority children*. Final Report to the Walter S. Johnson Foundation. Stanford, Calif.: Stanford University, School of Education.

Coleman, J. S. 1966. *Equality of educational opportunity*. Washington, D.C.: U.S. Government Printing Office.

Comer, J. P.; Schraft, C. M.; and Sparrow, S. S. 1980. *A social studies curriculum for inner city children: Final report*. New Haven, Conn.: Yale Child Study Center.

Committee for Economic Development. 1987. *Children in need: Investment strategies for the educationally disadvantaged*. Washington, D.C.: the Committee.

Cooper, K. J. 1987. Hispanic population grows 30% in 7 years. *Philadelphia Inquirer*, 11 July, 12C.

Copple, C.; Sigel, I. E.; and Saunders, R. 1984. *Educating the young thinker: Classroom strategies for cognitive growth*. Hillsdale, N.J.: Lawrence Erlbaum Associates.

Costa, A. L. 1984. Mediating the metacognitive. *Educational Leadership* 42(3): 57–67.

Costa, A. L., ed. 1985. *Developing minds: A resource book for teaching thinking*. Alexandria, Va.: Association for Supervision and Curriculum Development.

Council for Economic Development. 1987. *Children in need: Strategies for the educationally disadvantaged*. New York: the Council.

Crawford, J. 1987. Bilingual education works, study finds. *Education Week* 6(26): 16.

Cuban, L. 1987. Schooling the at-risk child: Lessons for policymakers and practitioners. Paper presented at the North Central Regional Educational Laboratory Conference, Chicago. Photocopy.

Cummins, J. 1986. Empowering minority students: A framework for intervention. *Harvard Educational Review* 56(1): 18–36.

De Avila, E., and Duncan, S. 1985. The language-minority child: A psychological, linguistic, and social analysis. In *Thinking and learning skills*. Vol. 2, *Research and open questions*, ed. S. F. Chipman, J. W. Segal, and R. Glaser, 245–74. Hillsdale, N.J.: Lawrence Erlbaum Associates.

Deutsch, M., ed. 1967. *The disadvantaged child.* New York: Basic Books.

Deutsch, M. 1986. Book review of R. E. Slavin et al., eds., Learning to cooperate, cooperating to learn. *Teachers College Record* 87(4): 630–33.

Dewey, J. 1910. *How we think.* New York: D. C. Heath.

Dillon, R. F., and Sternberg, F. J. 1986. *Cognition and instruction.* Orlando, Fla.: Academic Press.

Durán, R. P. 1983. *Hispanics' education and background: Predictors of college achievement.* New York: College Entrance Examination Board.

Edmonds, R. 1986. Characteristics of effective schools. In *The school achievement of minority children: New perspectives*, ed. U. Neisser, 93–104. Hillsdale, N.J.: Lawrence Erlbaum Associates.

Educational Leadership. 1982. Special issue: More effective schools, 40(3).

Educational Researcher. 1983. Effective schools: A special issue with guest editor W. Bickel, 12(4).

Edwards, J., and Baldauf, R. B., Jr. 1987. A detailed analysis of CoRT-1 in classroom practice. Paper presented at the 3d International Conference on Thinking, Honolulu, Hawaii. Photocopy.

Eisner, E. W. 1987. The celebration of thinking. *Educational Horizons* 66(1): 24–29.

Elkind, D. 1976. *Child development and education: A Piagetian perspective.* New York: Oxford University Press.

Engs, R. F. 1987. Historical perspective on the problem of black literacy. *Educational Horizons* 66(1): 13–17.

Ennis, R. H. 1985. A logical basis for measuring critical thinking skills. *Educational Leadership* 43(2): 44–48.

Feuerstein, R. 1979. *The dynamic assessment of retarded performers: The learning potential assessment device, theory, instruments, and techniques.* Glenview, Ill.: Scott, Foresman.

Feuerstein, R. 1980. *Instrumental enrichment: An intervention program for cognitive modifiability.* In collaboration with Y. Rand, M. B. Hoffman, and R. Miller. Baltimore, Md.: University Park Press.

Feuerstein, R. 1981. Mediated learning experiences in the acquisition of kinesics. In *Developmental kinesics: The emerging paradigm*, ed. B. L. Hoffer and R. N. St. Clair, 91–106. Baltimore, Md.: University Park Press.

Feuerstein, R.; Jensen, M. R.; Hoffman, M. B.; and Rand, Y. 1985. Instrumental enrichment, an intervention program for structural cognitive modifiability: Theory and practice. In *Thinking and learning skills*. Vol. 1, *Relating instruction to research*, ed. J. W. Segal, S. F. Chipman, and R. Glaser, 43–82. Hillsdale, N.J.: Lawrence Erlbaum Associates.

Fine, M. 1986. Why urban adolescents drop into and out of public high school. *Teachers College Record* 87(3): 393–409.

Gannon, K. E., and Ginsburg, H. P. 1985. Children's learning difficulties in mathematics. *Education and Urban Society* 17(4): 405–16.

Garber, H., and Heber, R. 1982. Modification of predicted cognitive development in high-risk children through early intervention. In *How and how much can intelligence be increased,* ed. D. K. Detterman and R. J. Sternberg, 121–37. Norwood, N.J.: Ablex.

Gay, G. 1975. Cultural differences important in education of Black children. *Momentum* 6(3): 30–33.

Gersten, R., and Keating, T. 1987. Long-term benefits from direct instruction. *Educational Leadership* 44(6): 28–31.

Gilbert, S. E., II, and Gay, G. 1985. Improving the success in school of poor Black children. *Phi Delta Kappan* 67(2): 133–37.

Ginsburg, H. P. 1972. *The myth of the deprived child: Poor children's intellect and education.* Englewood Cliffs, N.J.: Prentice-Hall.

Ginsburg, H. P. 1986. The myth of the deprived child: New thoughts on poor children. In *The school achievement of minority children: New perspectives,* ed. U. Neisser, 169–89. Hillsdale, N.J.: Lawrence Erlbaum Associates.

Glaser, R. 1984. Education and thinking: The role of knowledge. *American Psychologist* 39(2): 93–104.

Gold, D. L. 1987. English-immersion students perform well in study. *Education Week* 7(3): 5.

Good, T. L. 1987. Two decades of research on teacher expectations: Findings and future directions. *Journal of Teacher Education* 38(4): 32–47.

Hakuta, K. 1986. *Mirror of language: The debate on bilingualism.* New York: Basic Books.

Hakuta, K., and Diaz, R. M. 1985. The relationship between degree of bilingualism and cognitive ability: A critical discussion and some new longitudinal data. In *Children's language.* Vol. 5, ed. K. E. Nelson. Hillsdale, N.J.: Lawrence Erlbaum Associates.

Hakuta, K., and Gould, L. 1987. Synthesis of research on bilingual education. *Educational Leadership* 44(6): 38–45.

Hamilton, S. F. 1986. Raising standards and reducing dropout rates. *Teachers College Record* 87(3): 410–29.

Hammack, F. M. 1986. Large school systems' dropout reports: An analysis of definitions, procedures, and findings. *Teachers College Record* 87(3): 324–41.

Harris, T. L., and Cooper, E. J., eds. 1985. *Reading, thinking, and concept development: Strategies for the classroom.* New York: College Entrance Examination Board.

Haywood, C. 1986. Teachers as mediators. *Human Intelligence International Newsletter* 7(1): 3.

Herrnstein, R. J.; Nickerson, R. S.; de Sanchez, M.; and Swets, J. A. 1986. Teaching thinking skills. *American Psychologist* 41(11): 1279–89.

Hochman, G. 1987. Overcoming dyslexia. *Philadelphia Inquirer Magazine,* 12 July, 12–17, 25–26, 28, 35.

Hodgkinson, H. L. 1985. *All one system: Demographics of education, kindergarten through graduate school.* Washington, D.C.: Institute for Educational Leadership.

Institute for the Advancement of Philosophy for Children. 1986. *Philosophy for children: Where are we now....* Upper Montclair, N.J.: the Institute.

Jensen, A. R. 1969. How much can we boost IQ and scholastic achievement? *Harvard Educational Review* 39(1): 1–123.

Jensen, A. R. 1981. Obstacles, problems, and pitfalls in differential psychology. In *Race, social class, and individual differences in I.Q.*, ed. S. Scarr. Hillsdale, N.J.: Lawrence Erlbaum Associates.

Jensen, A. R. 1985. Compensatory education and the theory of intelligence. *Phi Delta Kappan* 66(8): 554–58.

Jensen, A. R. 1986. *g*: Artifact or reality? *Journal of Vocational Behavior* 29(3): 301–31.

Johnson, D. W. 1981. Student-student interaction: The neglected variable in education. *Educational Researcher* 10(1): 5–10.

Jones, B. F. 1986. Quality and equality through cognitive instruction. *Educational Leadership* 43(7): 5–11.

Jones, B. F., and Friedman, L. B. 1987. *Active instruction for students at risk: Remarks on merging process-outcome and cognitive perspectives*. Elmhurst, Ill.: North Central Regional Educational Laboratory. Photocopy.

Jones, B. F.; Palincsar, A. S.; Ogle, D. S.; and Carr, E. G., eds. 1987. *Strategic teaching and learning: Cognitive instruction in the content areas*. Alexandria, Va.: Association for Supervision and Curriculum Development.

Juel, C.; Griffith, P. L.; and Gough, P. B. 1986. Acquisition of literacy: A longitudinal study of children in first and second grade. *Journal of Educational Psychology* 78(4): 243–55.

Kamii, C. 1984. Autonomy: The aim of education envisioned by Piaget. *Phi Delta Kappan* 65(6): 410–15.

Knoll, M. K. 1987. Foreword. In *Strategic teaching and learning: Cognitive instruction in the content areas*, ed. B. F. Jones, A. S. Palincsar, D. S. Ogle, and E. G. Carr, vii–viii. Alexandria, Va.: Association for Supervision and Curriculum Development.

Kuhn, D. 1986. Education for thinking. *Teachers College Record* 87(4): 495–512.

Labov, W. 1972. *Language in the inner city*. Philadelphia: University of Pennsylvania Press.

Laosa, L. M. 1977. Socialization, education, and continuity: The importance of sociocultural context. *Young Children* 32(5): 21–27.

Laosa, L. M. 1979. Inequality in the classroom: Observational research on teacher-student interactions. *Aztlan International Journal of Chicano Studies Research* 8:51–67.

Laosa, L. M. 1984. Ethnic, socioeconomic, and home language influences upon early performance on measures of ability. *Journal of Educational Psychology* 76(6): 1178–98.

Levin, H. M. 1986. *Educational reform for disadvantaged students: An emerging crisis*. Washington, D.C.: National Education Association.

Levin, H. M. 1987. Accelerated schools for disadvantaged students. *Educational Leadership* 44(6): 19–21.

Levine, D. U.; Holdsworth, S.; and Aquila, F. D. 1987. Achievement gains in self-contained Chapter 1 classes in Kansas City. *Educational Leadership* 44(6): 22–23.

Link, F. R. 1985. Instrumental enrichment: A strategy for cognitive and academic improvement. In *Essays on the intellect*, ed. F. R. Link, 89–106. Alexandria, Va.: Association for Supervision and Curriculum Development.

Lipman, M.; Sharp, A. M.; and Oscanyan, F. S. 1980. *Philosophy in the classroom*. Philadelphia: Temple University Press.

Lipson, M. Y., and Wixson, K. K. 1986. Reading disability research: An interactionist perspective. *Review of Educational Research* 56(1): 111–36.

McDill, E. L.; Natriello, G.; and Pallas, A. M. 1986. A population at risk: Potential consequences of tougher school standards for student dropouts. *American Journal of Education* 94(2): 135–81.

Mann, D. 1986. Can we help dropouts? Thinking about the undoable. *Teachers College Record* 87(3): 307–23.

Martin, J. F., and Weinstein, M. L. 1984. *Thinking skills and philosophy for children: The Bethlehem Program, 1982–1983*. Bethlehem, Pa.: Bethlehem Area School District. Photocopy.

Marzano, R. J.; Brandt, R.; Hughes, C.; Jones, B. F.; Presseisen, B. Z.; Rankin, S.; and Suhor, C. 1988. *Dimensions of thinking: A framework for curriculum and instruction*. Alexandria, Va.: Association for Supervision and Curriculum Development.

Marzano, R. J., and Hutchins, C. L. 1985. *Thinking skills: A conceptual framework*. Aurora, Colo., and Kansas City, Mo.: Mid-Continent Regional Educational Laboratory.

Meyers, C. 1986. *Teaching students to think critically*. San Francisco: Jossey-Bass.

Mezzacappa, D. 1987a. City dropout study paints grim picture. *Philadelphia Inquirer*, 5 July, 1A, 6A.

Mezzacappa, D. 1987b. Learning in two languages: Advantage or hindrance. *Philadelphia Inquirer*, 6 October, 20–21 HC.

Mezzacappa, D. 1987c. Gift of schooling may be hard to accept. *Philadelphia Inquirer*, 1 November, 1B, 6B.

Miller, J. A. 1987. Rights panel study says desegregation has been effective. *Education Week* 6(35): 1, 18.

Montague, B. 1987. Chicago business heads take hands-on approach to reform. *Education Week* 7(4): 1, 19.

National Assessment of Educational Progress. 1987. National effort needed to raise the quality of literacy in America. *ETS Developments* 33(1): 2.

National Coalition of Advocates for Students. 1985. *Barriers to excellence: Our children at risk*. Boston: the Coalition.

National Commission on Excellence in Education. 1983. *A nation at risk: The imperative for educational reform*. Washington, D.C.: U.S. Government Printing Office.

National Commission on Secondary Education for Hispanics. 1984. *Making something happen: Hispanics and urban high school reform*. 2 vols. Washington, D.C.: Hispanic Policy Development Project.

Neisser, U., ed. 1986. *The school achievement of minority children: New perspectives*. Hillsdale, N.J.: Lawrence Erlbaum Associates.

New York Times. 1987. Dyslexia's cause is reportedly found. 13 January, C1.

Nickerson, R. S. 1984. Kinds of thinking taught in current programs. *Educational Leadership* 42(1): 26–36.

Nickerson, R. S. 1986a. Project Intelligence: An account and some reflections. In *Facilitating cognitive development: International perspectives, programs, and practices*, ed. M. Schwebel and C. A. Maher. New York: Haworth Press.

Nickerson, R. S. 1986b. Reasoning. In *Cognition and instruction*, ed. R. F. Dillon and R. J. Sternberg, 343–73. Orlando, Fla.: Academic Press.

Ogbu, J. U. 1978. *Minority education and caste: The American system in cross-cultural perspective.* New York: Academic Press.

Ogbu, J. U. 1986. The consequences of the American caste system. In *The school achievement of minority children: New perspectives*, ed. U. Neisser, 19–56. Hillsdale, N.J.: Lawrence Erlbaum Associates.

Olson, L. 1987. Coalition of educators urges wider efforts for "at-risk" youths. *Education Week* 6(37): 1, 12.

Orr, E. W. 1987. *Twice as less: Black English and the performance of Black students in mathematics and science.* New York: W. W. Norton.

Palincsar, A. S., and Brown, A. L. 1984. Reciprocal teaching of comprehension-fostering and comprehension-monitoring activities. *Cognition and Instruction* 1(2): 117–75.

Perfetti, C. A. 1984. Reading acquisition and beyond: Decoding includes cognition. *American Journal of Education* 93(1): 40–60.

Pifer, A. 1979. Bilingual education and the Hispanic challenge. *1979 annual report.* New York: Carnegie Corporation.

Pittman, R. B. 1986. The importance of personal, social factors as potential means for reducing high school dropout rate. *The High School Journal* 70(1): 7–13.

Portes, P. R. 1985. The role of language in the development of intelligence: Vygotsky revisited. *Journal of Research and Development in Education* 18(4): 1–10.

Presseisen, B. Z. 1985. *Unlearned lessons: Current and past reforms for school improvement.* Philadelphia and London: Falmer Press, Taylor and Francis Group.

Presseisen, B. Z. 1986. *Critical thinking and thinking skills: State of the art definitions and practice in public schools.* Philadelphia: Research for Better Schools.

Presseisen, B. Z. 1987. *Thinking skills throughout the curriculum: A conceptual design.* Bloomington, Ind.: Pi Lambda Theta.

Report on Education Research. 1987. Hispanics face growing isolation in schools, researchers say. 19(17): 7–8.

Resnick, L. B. 1985. *Education and learning to think.* Pittsburgh: University of Pittsburgh, Learning Research and Development Center. Photocopy.

Rosenthal, R., and Jacobson, L. 1968. *Pygmalion in the classroom: Teacher expectation and pupils' intellectual development.* New York: Holt, Rinehart & Winston.

Rumberger, R. W. 1987. High school dropouts: A review of issues and evidence. *Review of Educational Research* 57(2): 101–21.

Russell, R. L., and Ginsburg, H. P. 1984. Cognitive analysis of children's mathematics difficulties. *Cognition and Instruction* 1(2): 217–44.

Samway, K. D., and Alvarez, L. P. 1987. Integrating language arts instruction for language minority students. *Educational Horizons* 66(1): 20–23.

Savell, J. M.; Twohig, P. T.; and Rachford, D. L. 1986. Empirical status of Feuerstein's "Instrumental Enrichment" (FIE) technique as a method of teaching thinking skills. *Review of Educational Research* 56(4): 381–409.

Schweinhart, L. J., and Weikart, D. P. 1985. Evidence that good early childhood programs work. *Phi Delta Kappan* 66(8): 545–53.

Sewell, T. E. 1987. Dynamic assessment as a nondiscriminatory procedure. In *Dynamic assessment*, ed. C. S. Lidz. New York: Guilford Publications.

Shipman, V. C. 1982. Evaluation of the Philosophy for Children Program in Bethlehem, Pennsylvania. *Thinking* 4(1): 37–40.

Shulman, L. S. 1986. Those who understand: Knowledge growth in teaching. *Educational Researcher* 15(2): 4–14.

Shulman, L. S. 1987. Knowledge and teaching: Foundations of the new reform. *Harvard Educational Review* 57(1): 1–22.

Slavin, R. E. 1980. Cooperative learning. *Review of Educational Research* 50(2): 315–42.

Slavin, R. E. 1981. Synthesis of research on cooperative learning. *Educational Leadership* 38(8): 655–60.

Slavin, R. E. 1987. Making Chapter 1 make a difference. *Phi Delta Kappan* 69(2): 110–19.

Slavin, R. E.; Karweit, N. L.; and Madden, N. A. 1987. *Success for all: A proposal for elementary school reform*. Baltimore, Md.: Johns Hopkins University, Center for Research on Elementary and Middle Schools. Photocopy.

Stallings, J. 1981. Effective strategies for teaching basic skills. In *Developing basic skills programs in secondary schools*, ed. D. G. Wallace, 1–19. Washington, D.C.: Association for Supervision and Curriculum Development.

Stern, M. J. 1987. The welfare of families. *Educational Leadership* 44(6): 82–87.

Sternberg, R. J. 1981. Intelligence as thinking and learning skills. *Educational Leadership* 39(1): 18–20.

Sternberg, R. J. 1983. Criteria for intellectual skills training. *Educational Researcher* 12(2): 6–12, 26.

Sternberg, R. J. 1984. How can we teach intelligence? *Educational Leadership* 42(1): 38–48.

Sternberg, R. J. 1985a. Choosing the right program. In *Developing minds: A resource book for teaching thinking*, ed. A. L. Costa, 185–86. Alexandria, Va.: Association for Supervision and Curriculum Development.

Sternberg, R. J. 1985b. Critical thinking: Its nature, measurement, and improvement. In *Essays on the intellect*, ed. F. R. Link, 45–65. Alexandria, Va.: Association for Supervision and Curriculum Development.

Sternberg, R. J. 1986. Cognition and instruction: Why the marriage sometimes ends in divorce. In *Cognition and instruction*, ed. R. F. Dillon and R. J. Sternberg, 375–82. Orlando, Fla.: Academic Press.

Sternberg, R. J. 1987. Teaching critical thinking: Eight easy ways to fail. *Phi Delta Kappan* 68(6): 456–59.

Sternberg, R. J., and Bhana, K. 1986. Synthesis of research on the effectiveness of intellectual skills programs: Snake-oil remedies or miracle cures? *Educational Leadership* 44(2): 60–67.

Strother, D. B. 1986. Dropping out. *Phi Delta Kappan* 68(4): 325–28.

Vygotsky, L. S. 1962. *Thought and language*. Translated and edited by E. Hanfmann and G. Vakar. Cambridge, Mass.: MIT Press.

Wassermann, S. 1987. Teaching for thinking: Louis E. Raths revisited. *Phi Delta Kappan* 68(6): 460–66.

Wehlage, G. G., and Rutter, R. A. 1986. Evaluation of a model program for at-risk high school students. Paper presented at the annual meeting of the American Educational Research Association, San Francisco.

Wehlage, G. G.; Rutter, R. A.; and Turnbaugh, A. 1987. A program model for at-risk high school students. *Educational Leadership* 44(6): 70–73.

Wehlage, G. G.; Stone, C.; and Lesko, N. 1982. *Effective programs for the marginal high school student: A report to the Wisconsin governor's employment and training office.* Madison: Wisconsin Center for Education Research, University of Wisconsin–Madison.

Whimbey, A., and Whimbey, L. S. 1975. *Intelligence can be taught.* New York: E. P. Dutton.

Willis, H. D. 1986. *Students at risk: A review of conditions, circumstances, indicators, and educational implications.* Elmhurst, Ill.: North Central Regional Educational Laboratory.

Wilson, W. J. 1987. *The truly disadvantaged: The inner-city, the underclass, and public policy.* Chicago: University of Chicago Press.

Worsham, A. M., and Stockton, A. J. 1985. *A model for teaching thinking skills: The inclusion process.* Bloomington, Ind.: Phi Delta Kappa Educational Foundation.

Yankelovich, Skelly, and White, Inc. 1984. *Spanish USA 1984.* New York: the Author.

Zinner, J. 1985. Thinking makes an impact. *Thrust for Educational Leadership* 14(7): 30–32.

4. LEARNING AND ASSISTED PERFORMANCE

by Richard P. Durán

What makes school learning so problematical for some students and not for others? This question has proved difficult to answer, and especially so for students from ethnic and racial minority backgrounds. The poor school performance of minority students cannot be traced to a single cause; nor does the solution to this problem lie ultimately in a single answer. Nonetheless, improving the quality of minority students' classroom experiences is a critical element in improving their educational outcomes. Over the past two decades, research evidence has begun to accumulate indicating that minority students learn best when instruction and teaching are sensitive to their linguistic, social, and cultural knowledge. More recently, researchers have investigated the acquisition of cognitive skills and literacy as a function of these factors. This chapter discusses some of these findings and how they are illuminated by a recent account of teaching and learning based on the notion of "assisted performance" (Tharp and Gallimore 1988). The chapter also discusses the importance of designing and evaluating school interventions that develop minority students' academic and personal identity across tiers of the educational system. This latter issue has not yet been adequately dealt with by theories of educational intervention for at-risk minority students.

CLASSROOMS AS SOCIAL ENVIRONMENTS

Ethnographic studies of minority students' classroom behavior have shown that their classroom performance is very much affected by their norms for communication in and out of school settings. Simply put, students cannot be taught well and they cannot learn effectively when classroom communication patterns are unfamiliar to them. Several findings in the research literature deserve mention. One is that minority students' preferred manner of interacting with teachers and students may, at times, mistakenly indicate that these students are poor learners. For example, culturally preferred styles of interaction may lead some minority students to be unresponsive to a teacher's questions in a public classroom setting (Carrasco, Vera, and Cazden 1981; Phillips 1972). Another finding is that the structure of the curriculum and communication patterns fostered in low-achieving classroom tracks may deter minority students from effectively learning higher-order reading and thinking skills (Oakes 1985). For example, practicing the pronunciation of isolated words in the second language is not as effective in developing reading comprehension skills as is writing a book report in the first language (Moll et al. 1980). Yet another important finding is that by connecting classroom learning activities with minority students' knowledge of out-of-school experiences and peer communication norms, we can improve their learning performance in areas such as reading and other forms of literacy acquisition (Au et al. 1986; Anderson and Stokes 1984; Heath 1983). Researchers at the Kamehameha Early Education Program (KEEP), for example, have found that small-group reading activities which allow children to explore story topics in light of their own experiences and which use communicative patterns learned in the community help cultivate students' comprehension skills (Au et al. 1986).

Making sense of these interrelated results and their implications for designing educational interventions for at-risk students requires a more encompassing account of how social factors can affect classroom organization and classroom behavior. Such an examination lies at the heart of curriculum and instruction planning in the school setting.

Classroom organization and student performance are affected by three general kinds of social factors (Erickson 1982). The first group of social factors includes the overall societal and cultural context of schooling and the purposes served by schools as institutions within the country, the state, and the community. This societal-level factor is diffuse, although its effects on education are pervasive. It encompasses the values and attitudes of educational policymakers and the impact their values and attitudes have on how schools operate and how resources are allocated within a system. In addition, this factor encompasses the general public's attitudes about why schooling is important, the extent to which schooling is expected to serve students from different backgrounds equally well, and the willingness of citizens to allocate public resources for the purposes of education.

This factor also encompasses minority students' beliefs that schooling is appropriate for them as minority group members, based on the beliefs of others as well as on their own experiences. A teacher's belief that members of certain minority groups are innately socially and intellectually inferior can be translated in classroom contexts into lowered expectations for educational performance. Minority students themselves, and particularly those from impoverished homes, may judge that good school performance is less likely to promote their familial, financial, and personal well-being as compared to nonminority students (Ogbu and Matute-Bianchi 1985).

A second social factor affecting classroom organization is the immediate school environment itself and how it is structured and operates. The meaning of this factor is captured by the ways in which the following

66

questions might be answered: What curricula are taught, and what are students asked to do in order to learn these curricula? What books do teachers use? How compatible are the curricula, materials, and books used with students' backgrounds and previous educational experiences? What is the nature of the school day, and how are different learning activities distributed across the time spent at school? Are students tracked into ability groups based on their past school achievement? Answers to these questions can help describe the school environment faced by at-risk minority students. They can also suggest whether students are truly being given an opportunity to learn from the school's program.

A third form of social influence on classroom organization pertains to the behaviors of the teacher and the minority student learners as instruction actually takes place. This third factor is both social and psychological. It is social because the classroom behavior of the teacher and the students is intimately influenced by their social background, the social interaction required by the learning activities, and the social management provided by the teacher. The factor is psychological in that it reflects the values, attitudes, motivations, and cognitive processes of individual learners and of the teacher as they arise in classroom interaction.

Our understanding of how this third factor operates is enhanced by closer consideration of how a classroom's teaching and learning activities are structured. As Erickson (1982) has noted, the teacher's and students' enactment of a lesson is structured by both the teacher's lesson plan and the social interaction requirements of the lesson. As a lesson proceeds, the teacher and students monitor and adjust their behavior, given the teacher's enactment of a plan for the lesson. The teacher and students jointly construct and revise their pattern of communication as the learning activity develops, in light of the teacher's monitoring of students' understanding of the subject matter content and relative to the social knowledge shared by the teacher and students about how to communicate.

THE ASSISTED PERFORMANCE THEORY

The fact that learning opportunities arise through social interaction in the classroom has important implications for our understanding of the academic functioning of at-risk students. We need to examine carefully whether teacher/student interactions truly permit these students to learn. Tharp and Gallimore (1988) have proposed an account of teaching and learning that is of special relevance to this question. Drawing on Vygotsky's (1978) notion of "the zone of proximal development," these researchers propose that true teaching can occur only when a teacher or more capable other assists the performance of a student so that the student advances through his or her zone of proximal development for the learning task at hand.

Let us examine this account more carefully and in more detail in order to understand its relevance for at-risk students. In his theory of cognitive development, Vygotsky (1978) defined the zone of proximal development as—

> ... the distance between the actual developmental level as determined by individual problem solving and the level of potential development as determined through problem solving under adult guidance or in collaboration with more capable peers. (p. 86)

The zone of proximal development has a clear intuitive meaning. Given a particular problem-solving task, this zone is identified by those parts of the problem-solving act that are beyond the ability of a person to carry out independently, but that a person is capable of carrying out with sufficient assistance from a teacher or more capable other.

The singular goal of all teaching is to assist the learner in cultivating an independent ability to perform a problem-solving task that was previously unattainable by that learner. We can say teaching occurs only when the teacher or more capable other assists the student in performing a previously unattainable element of a problem-solving task. This is a very strong criterion for defining the occurrence of teaching. Implicitly, if not explicitly, it requires (1) that the teacher possess an understanding of the current capabilities of the student, (2) that the teacher be able to select and provide cues and hints that aid the student's learning, and (3) that the teacher be able to evaluate the student's responses to hints and cues, and to use this information to evaluate the student's mastery of the problem-solving task at hand. Further, (4) in providing hints and cues, the teacher must be capable of guiding the student toward less reliance on externally generated cues and hints and toward more independence in solving problems.

The learner's progress through the zone of proximal development for a problem-solving task occurs in four stages (see Figure 1). During Stage I, a learner can execute a problem-solving task only when he or she is assisted at various points by a more capable other. Subsequently, in Stage II, the learner has begun to internalize the cues and helpful modes of approaching the problem-solving task required during Stage I. During this stage, he or she consciously applies these internalized strategies and begins to perform the problem-solving task independently.

Movement of the learner from Stage I into Stage II embodies the Vygotskian principle that higher-order cognitive functioning first arises in the social plane of experience and then, subsequently, becomes

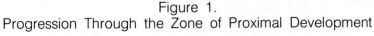

Figure 1.
Progression Through the Zone of Proximal Development

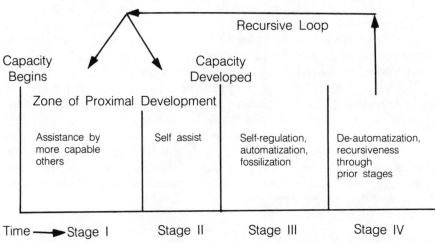

Source: Adapted from Tharp, R., and Gallimore, R. 1988. *Rousing minds to life: Teaching, learning and schooling in social context.* Cambridge, England: Cambridge University Press.

internalized as a form of "inner speech" within the individual. The self-assistance generated by the learner in Stage II is a metacognitive phenomenon. That is, as the learner attempts a problem-solving task, she or he encounters difficulties that must be resolved by consciously analyzing the demands of the task at hand, by monitoring progress on the task, and by evaluating and trying out different strategies to overcome the difficulties. At first, the student's metacognitive behavior directly models the hints and cues provided by the more competent other during Stage I. Gradually, as the learner moves from Stage II to Stage III, she or he develops increasing competence in performing the problem-solving task and relies less on consciously modeling the specific cues and hints generated originally by the more capable other. Instead, the learner becomes more reliant on her/his own internally generated ways of approaching and carrying out the task.

By the time he or she reaches Stage III, the learner has developed a highly automated approach toward performing a problem-solving task. In this stage, the learner is able to recognize quickly what is required in performing a problem-solving act and to engage in the necessary strategic behavior with minimal conscious reflection and uncertainty. In Stage III, the learner engages in problem-solving behavior automatically under the regulation of a well-identified sense of what constitutes progress on a task and of how to go about performing it. Problem solving in Stage III can be characterized as a "fossilized" form of knowledge in that the learner no longer questions actively how a problem should be interpreted and approached. He or she relies on previous experience and prior knowledge to approach the familiar tasks.

Once a learner has achieved Stage III, she or he may not remain there permanently. What has been learned and automated in Stage III may become unstable or may be judged inadequate knowledge as a result of either normal memorial decay processes or new experiences that point to inadequacies in prior learning or approaches. The need for the learner to modify previous Stage III learning is represented by Stage IV in Tharp and Gallimore's model. During Stage IV, the learner returns to either Stage I or Stage II in order to engage in new learning. In the suggested model, this recursion through Stages I, II, and III may become cascaded. The recursion represents the potential of the learner to acquire new knowledge and skills based on a restructuring of old knowledge throughout her or his life span.

TEACHING STRATEGIES

Many everyday classroom situations are characterized by the students' presence in Stage I of their zone of proximal development. An important question that arises is, What different strategies can a teacher or more capable other use to assist the problem-solving performance of a learner? Based on the Tharp and Gallimore model, the following strategies may assist the performance of the learner in Stage I:

- *Modeling*: Offering behavior for imitation.
- *Contingency managing*: Arranging rewards or punishments to follow a particular behavior, depending on whether the behavior is desired or not.
- *Feeding back*: Providing performance information to the learner relative to standards for performance.
- *Instructing*: Using language to call for a specific action on the part of the learner.
- *Questioning*: Using questions to assess the current knowledge state of the learner and/or to assist the learner in performing a particular mental operation.
- *Cognitive structuring*: Providing the learner with systems of ideas to explain and articulate knowledge or to organize cognitive activity.

The foregoing list of teaching strategies can be used to study the effective behaviors of teachers. It also has implications for teacher preparation. Each strategy must be competently performed by the teacher, and, in turn, students must recognize the occurrence of a strategy and what it demands of them within the social and academic contexts of a lesson. A further issue is whether the use of a particular strategy actually helps a student advance through his/her zone of proximal development for a task. Teachers must be given an opportunity to develop skill in knowing when and how to use different strategies during instruction. It would appear that these skills, and knowing how to deploy them, would best be learned through actual teaching experiences, with help and feedback provided by competent teacher trainers. As Tharp and Gallimore (1988) note, the assisted performance mode of teaching and learning can be applied to teachers learning their craft, as well as to students learning from teachers (Chapter 9).

The appropriateness of the various teaching strategies for students from different sociocultural and linguistic backgrounds is an important question. Current everyday wisdom and research suggest the effectiveness of a given teaching strategy may vary across groups of students from different backgrounds who are performing the same learning tasks. For example, using questioning and cognitive structuring during a small-group reading comprehension activity works with Navajo children only when the group size is small—three to four children; by comparison, such strategies are successful with Hawaiian-origin children in larger groups of five to six youngsters (Au et al. 1986).

The question of how best to select strategies for teaching minority students is complex. Seemingly the best answer to the question is that teachers need to learn how to adapt to the students they actually encounter in classrooms. Based on the characteristics of the students they work with, teachers need to develop professional wisdom about the social and cultural abilities of students that might be used as bridges to classroom learning and that might be compatible with particular teaching strategies. Further, teachers need to develop strategies for helping students expand their repertoire of classroom learning behaviors. Students, and particularly at-risk students, need to develop multiple ways of learning in a classroom. In particular, as they advance through their schooling, students need to develop increasing self-reliance in monitoring their own learning needs, and they need to adapt to the teaching they encounter.

ADDITIONAL IMPLICATIONS FOR
AT-RISK MINORITY STUDENTS

The fact that many at-risk minority students are not learning in everyday classroom learning activities is self-evident. The assisted performance account of learning and teaching suggests that many classroom activities encountered by at-risk minority students do not permit true teaching to occur, in the sense that students are not aided in progressing

71

from Stage I into Stage II of Tharp and Gallimore's model. This interpretation of educational failure is consistent with the sociolinguistic and ethnographic research literature cited with regard to the learning of minority students (Ogbu and Matute-Bianchi 1985).

The assisted performance account of learning and teaching, however, advances the design, implementation, and evaluation of interventions for minority students. Under assisted performance theory, an important educational intervention goal is to create learning activities that can ensure students' progress through the zone of proximal development in a particular subject matter or in a specific problem-solving area. Obviously, knowledge about the students' abilities is essential, as is understanding of the structure of the knowledge involved and its development for the learners.

Based on theory, one would judge that whole-group instruction, emphasizing lecturing by a teacher who then addresses questions to the entire group of students, would be particularly ineffective for at-risk students. In most whole-group settings, the teacher introduces and communicates content material without actively monitoring whether *each* student adequately comprehends it. When a teacher asks questions, students who are allowed to respond are selected from those who raise their hands. Because of this, the teacher has no opportunity to evaluate the learning needs of students who do not volunteer to respond or who might want to ask a question before volunteering. All too often, if a student does not answer a question as desired, the teacher will not probe the understanding of the learner; nor will he/she offer cues to guide the learner to the desired response. Instead, the teacher may simply call on one student after another until one elicits the desired response to the question at hand.

This whole-group instruction technique is not ineffective for all students. As students become more proficient in their learning (e.g., as they enter Stages II and III of learning), they can actually benefit from such instruction. However, at-risk students very often are functioning in the model's Stage I of learning. They are simply incapable of working on the task without the assistance of a more capable other. It is disastrous not to acknowledge this possibility for these youngsters. Students who are in Stage I may be "taught at," but they cannot learn very well under the circumstances that exist. That is not to say they do not have potential for learning.

Cooperative learning methods, an alternative to whole-group instruction methods, would seem more effective for teaching at-risk minority students (Kagan 1986). These methods stimulate learning among students by requiring them to cooperate and collaborate in the performance of learning tasks. While a number of cooperative learning models exists, the underlying instructional theory for all these methods

72

emphasizes the use of "awards" as learning incentives. A recent synthesis of research on cooperative learning indicates the most effective methods emphasize group goals coupled with individual student accountability (Slavin in preparation). In addition to improving student achievement, cooperative learning methods have also been found to foster interethnic/racial group relations, helping, and other prosocial behaviors in the classroom.

Cooperative learning methods have not yet been analyzed from the perspective of the assisted performance theory. Slavin (1987) suggests that Vygotskian and Piagetian theories of learning are not adequate to explain the success of cooperative learning methods because these two developmental theories do not properly conceptualize the motivation necessary for students to engage in learning. According to his research, Slavin proposes these theories postulate that students' intrinsic motivation to learn is adequate to sustain learning. However, studies of cooperative learning methods indicate that explicit use of performance awards leads to improved achievement by groups and individuals. Obviously, further research is needed.

The assisted performance theory, as a modification of Vygotsky's theory of learning, does address the importance of awards in supporting learning under the teaching strategy of contingency management. Pursuing this approach in classrooms of at-risk learners seems a promising practice in this era of school reform.

CROSS-TIER EDUCATIONAL INTERVENTIONS

Application of the assisted performance theory can lead to better conceptualization of interventions aimed at improving the short-range academic achievement of at-risk minority students. However, we should be able to extend the theory to address the development of the educational aspirations of these underachieving students. One key to devising such an extension is to use the assisted performance theory to characterize a student's modification of his or her social self-identity in light of long-range educational goals. A second key to devising aspiration-development interventions is to provide social/academic activities that allow role models, such as the teacher or a student at a higher grade level, to assist the at-risk student in acquiring an understanding of his or her life and personal values at the next educational tier. Consider, for example, devising activities that bring junior high students who are at risk of dropping out of school together with successful high school students from a similar background and with high school teachers who have shown competency in teaching minority students. These are the kinds of interventions that we need to address in schools in America's urban centers.

With proper care, we can devise cross-tier intervention activities that give at-risk students both needed academic instruction and information about the adaptive behavior and personal goals of students at the next educational tier. The general strategy for devising such cross-tier educational interventions would be to "manufacture" miniature social systems for the specific purpose of moving at-risk students through the educational pipeline. Research on cross-tier interventions from an assisted performance theory perspective has not yet been undertaken, but it is a most exciting prospect for enhancing the long-range educational achievement of at-risk minority students.

DISCUSSION QUESTIONS

1. How might minority students' communication patterns and performance norms influence their interaction with teachers in the classroom?

2. What potential classroom relationships are suggested by the concept of "zone of proximal development," and how are these relationships influenced by the classroom environmental decisions that teachers make?

3. Assisted performance is a model for helping students become more expert in the classroom; describe the states suggested by this model and explain how the teacher's role influences students' progress through such a model.

4. What kinds of teaching strategies or instructional techniques seem to be potentially effective in helping at-risk students become more cognitively skilled in the classroom?

REFERENCES

Anderson, A. B., and Stokes, S. J. 1984. Social and institutional influences on the development and practice of literacy. In *Awakening to literacy*, ed. F. Smith, H. Goelman, and A. Oberg, 24–37. New York: Heineman.

Au, K. H.; Crowell, D. C.; Jordan, C.; Sloat, K. C.; Speidel, G. E.; Klein, T. W.; and Tharp, R. G. 1986. Development and implementation of the KEEP reading program. In *Reading comprehension: From research to practice*, ed. J. Orasanu. Hillsdale, N.J.: Lawrence Erlbaum Associates.

Carrasco, R. L.; Vera, A.; and Cazden, C. 1981. Aspects of bilingual students' communicative competence in the classroom: A case study. In *Latino language and communicative behavior*, ed. R. Durán. Norwood, N.J.: Ablex Publishing Co.

Erickson, F. 1982. Taught cognitive learning in its immediate environments: A neglected topic in the anthropology of education. *Anthropology and Education Quarterly* 13(2): 149–80.

Heath, S. B. 1983. *Ways with words: Ethnography of communications in communities and classrooms*. New York: Cambridge University Press.

Kagan, S. 1986. Cooperative learning and sociocultural factors in schooling. In *Beyond language: Social and cultural factors in schooling language minority students*, ed. Bilingual Education Office. Los Angeles: California State University, Evaluation, Dissemination, and Assessment Center.

Moll, L.; Estrada, E.; Elette, E.; Diaz, E.; and Lopez, L. M. 1980. The construction of a learning environment in two languages. *The Quarterly Newsletter of the Laboratory of Comparative Human Cognition* 2(3): 53–58.

Oakes, J. 1985. *Keeping track: How schools structure inequality*. New Haven, Conn.: Yale University Press.

Ogbu, J., and Matute-Bianchi, M. 1985. Understanding sociocultural factors: Knowledge, identity and school adjustments. In *Beyond language: Social and cultural factors in schooling language minority students*, ed. Bilingual Education Office, 73–142. Los Angeles: California State University, Evaluation, Dissemination, and Assessment Center.

Phillips, S. 1972. Participant structures and communicative competence: Warm Springs children in community and classroom. In *Functions of language in the classroom*, ed. C. Cazden, D. Hymes, and V. John, 370–94. New York: Teachers College Press.

Slavin, R. E. 1987. Developmental and motivational perspectives on cooperative learning: A reconciliation. *Child Development* 58:1161–67.

Slavin, R. E. In preparation. Cooperative learning and student achievement. Baltimore, Md.: Center for Research on Elementary and Middle Schools, The Johns Hopkins University.

Tharp, R., and Gallimore, R. 1988. *Rousing minds to life: Teaching, learning, and schooling in social context*. Cambridge, England: Cambridge University Press.

Vygotsky, L. 1978. *Mind in society: The development of higher processes*, ed. M. Cole, V. John-Teiner, S. Scribner, and E. Souberonan. Cambridge, Mass.: Harvard University Press.

5. TOWARD REDEFINING MODELS OF CURRICULUM AND INSTRUCTION FOR STUDENTS AT RISK

by Beau Fly Jones

The current reform movement is ripe to address the needs of two types of at-risk students who really can't function in American society: disconnected youths and marginally skilled students. The concept of schooling itself needs to be expanded and coordinated with the work of many other organizations and agencies. More meaningful curriculum, instruction, and assessment, especially to encourage higher-order skill development, are called for. In addition, new ways to structure classroom organization, provide special services to students, and prevent major disaffection need to be developed. Such initiatives must be supported financially and legislatively, but also judged according to their success in terms of influencing students' lives. In order to do this, those practices that hold promise for at-risk students—like teaching thinking—need to be pursued, implemented, and researched further. No better climate for examination and experimentation may be available to American education for a long time to come.

The winds of change are finally here, heralding a new wave of reform that seeks sustained, fundamental change in schools, especially for students at risk. Phrases like "school renewal," "radical change," "parental/community involvement," "business/school partnerships," "systemic change," and "restructuring" are indeed refreshing and heartening. There is even an increasing focus on program improvement with a strong emphasis on curriculum and instruction, among the many initiatives and proposals supported by schools, state education agencies, and national groups.

Despite all these good recommendations for changes for students at risk, there are several concerns. First, there seems to be a lack of attention to the diverse needs of two types of at-risk students: (1) disconnected youths who are fundamentally alienated from basic American values and from economic and educational opportunities, and (2) semiskilled students who succeed in the basic skills programs assigned to them but who cannot read, write, or solve problems with proficiency and, therefore, can live only on the edges of mainstream society.

Second, given these problems, what can we do to address them? I believe that the concept of schooling needs to be expanded to include both direct instruction and support services in areas traditionally reserved for families and other social agencies. This approach also calls for the coordinated involvement of parents, senior citizens, civic workers, and the business community in schools as learners, teachers, role models, and providers of support services. Thus, in this conceptualization, schools serve multiple functions for students and for the community as learning centers for health care, child care and parent training, problem solving, and decision making in addition to offering instruction in the traditional disciplines.

Third, to what extent is the approach outlined here consistent with existing reform agendas? There is definitely support for most of the ideas in this extended-schooling approach in many recent reform initiatives and designs for future schools, but there are important gaps and limitations in the reform literature, especially regarding changes in curriculum and instruction.

Fourth, what are implications of the reform movement for curriculum and instruction? Specifically, it is argued that existing definitions of the role of students, teachers, instructional leaders, teacher educators, and curriculum and instruction constitute a poor foundation on which to support the reform agendas; new definitions are suggested to carry forward the intent of this wave of reform.

AT-RISK STUDENTS OVERLOOKED BY RECENT REFORMS

Who are the students, or would-be students, among the severely disconnected and the ranks of the semiskilled? What are their chances of leading productive lives within the context of mainstream America? How do the needs of these students for membership in the larger community and social bonding as well as thinking skills relate to the new reform movement? These questions guide the organization of this section.

Severely Disconnected Youth

The homeboys call him Frog. . . . He rakes in $200 a week selling crack, known as "rock" in East Los Angeles. He proudly advertises his fledgling membership in an ultra-violent street gang: the Crips. And he brags that he used his drug money to rent a Nissan Z on weekends. He has not yet learned how to use a stick shift, however, and at 4 ft. 10 in. he has trouble seeing over the dashboard. Frog is 13 years old. (Lamar 1988)

Frog is an example of the growing number of severely disconnected youths whose creative energies and entrepreneurial talents are adapted to survive in the underclass culture of drugs, street gangs, violence, crime, and prostitution (see also *Newsweek* 1988). While most children are at school, Frog and his peers are entrenched in the cross-fire of large-scale

77

political and corporate structures associated with the sale of drugs and arms nationally and internationally. Indeed, the powerful, rapid-fire Uzis and other weapons available to these youths seem far more frightening than the sawed-off shotguns and fire bombs of the Weathermen and race rioters of earlier decades. In a word, although these disconnected youths may be highly skilled in the jobs that define their world, they are *unskilled* in terms of the skills and knowledge needed to compete in mainstream occupations, and they are dangerous to society and, ultimately, to themselves. Moreover, their numbers are increasing; *Newsweek* (1988) estimates that the population of this underclass, which is largely minority, is about 2.5 million, roughly three times what it was in the 1970s.

Nor are all violent youths found emerging from poverty in our cities. Violent crimes among wealthy youths seem to be on the increase as well (Schorr and Schorr 1988). Drug use, drug dealing, alcoholism, violence, crime, and abuses arising from these activities have their counterparts among the very wealthy in cities and suburbs. Although the social and economic characteristics of these youths may be very different from those of inner city youths, they, too, are disconnected from their families, schools, religion, and other conventional social institutions. Thus, although these youths are not disadvantaged, we must consider their alienation as a parallel problem.

The needs of these disconnected youths are tremendous. Some of them need nourishing food, shelter, clothing, and medical services, especially if they are homeless, neglected, or abused. Many lack access to adequate and caring support services that would help them cope with poverty, personal distress and disaffection, family problems, peer pressure, and the dangers of the street. They need a curriculum that teaches them how to solve the problems they face and reconnects them to values for critical literacy and a level of meaningful participation in mainstream educational, political, and social processes. They need opportunities to be reconnected to jobs that have meaning, jobs that will provide them with hope for the future and chances for social mobility now unavailable to them. But, most important, they need access to people who care about them: people who have a stake in their future, people who believe they can learn to be successful citizens, workers, and members of the community.

The causes of their alienation and disconnection are complex and deeply rooted in the social, economic, and political fabric of the broader society—and certainly extend far beyond the scope of educational institutions. Educators clearly cannot deal with all of the problems; we must consider who is responsible for the education of these youths and what *can be done* by schools to provide better support services and education.

However, since these youths are so disconnected, I fear that their educational needs may fall through the cracks of the reform movement. Because they have committed crimes, some of these youths are in penal institutions that generally will not provide effective support services or education other than some basic skills and rudimentary training in a few trades. Consequently, when they leave, they may at best be able to read and write with minimal competence, but they are still disconnected from the mainstream of economic and political opportunities—not to mention the further disconnection caused by the crime and corruption that occurs inside penal institutions among the staff and the penal population. Because these youths are dangerous, many educators assume that they do not belong in school and plainly do not want them. And because they are largely dropouts, they fall outside most of the legislation intended for schools, except for dropout prevention programs, alternative schools, and reentry centers, which may be useful but are not sufficient.

More fundamental changes are needed to reclaim and harness into more productive channels the energy and creative talent that flow from these angry youths in the form of violent actions against society and, ultimately, against themselves.

Semiskilled Students

Harlow is a student at an inner-city high school that is rapidly improving its curriculum. However, when I met Harlow, he was essentially what I would call a semiskilled student. Although he was clearly bright and made good grades by his school's standards, he had little idea how to read or write with understanding, how to study complex expository materials, or how to solve academic problems beyond those in the book. His strategy for reading and studying was to read the questions at the end of the section or chapter and "scam" the text for the answers, a strategy that is typical of many learners (Anderson and Smith 1987). Harlow had no idea how the parts of a chapter were related, even though he could decode the words quite well and answer the questions with some accuracy. As of the second half of his sophomore year, he had never studied a whole chapter because he had never had a test covering more than a few pages or activities; nor was he ever required to integrate information from several chapters or units.

In contrast to Harlow, Marla attended a good high school in an all-white suburb that ranks high in number of students graduating and attending college. Although she was very bright and showed considerable potential in art and creative writing, she was tracked into lower-level classes because she was weak in mathematics and was often an impulsive learner. She was one of those students who would work hard and excel at tasks she found interesting and relevant to her life, but she was very undisciplined in her study habits, if the task had little immediate meaning. Marla also had a very low self-image and harbored a deep-seated hatred for school, stemming in part from the humiliation she felt at being in lower-track courses, in part from the watered-down curriculum she was offered, and in part from the social structure linked to the tracking system. After years of "fighting the system," Marla finally graduated but showed her ultimate bitterness by not attending her own graduation. Now she is struggling with the hardship of living on poor wages and coping with the realities of her limited occupational options. The irony is that if she had failed a few courses, she would have been offered a range of special services and instruction that might have changed her pattern of low achievement. On the other hand, when such services are offered in the context of tracking, there is great stigma associated with using them, so the services might have been just one more thing for her to fight.

There are literally millions of students like Marla and Harlow who have good, even excellent, capabilities and potential, but who may or may not finish high school and probably will not be able to compete for challenging jobs with reasonable earnings. Without intervention, these students at best may compete for the rapidly decreasing number of semiskilled jobs that require basic skills; but they could not compete well for the range of service jobs and information-processing occupations that require problem solving, skilled literacy, and knowledge of technology. At worst, they may fall into the ranks of the underclass. With appropriate intervention, they may approximate the patterns of achievement of more advantaged students (Levin 1976; Neisser 1986; Rohwer 1971).

While I believe other types of students at risk would benefit from the fundamental changes brought about by reform, in this chapter I chose to focus on semiskilled students for several reasons. First, I believe that these students might escape being defined as students at risk: Harlow, because he makes good grades in a school with relatively low standards; and Marla, because by tracking her into low-level courses, the school feels that it is serving her needs. Second, I believe that there is something dreadfully wrong with a definition of basic skills that does not include the critical literacy and problem-solving skills that students need for tomorrow's jobs. Thus, I would seriously question the success of school improvement efforts that move students at risk from the 30th percentile to the 40th, or to some other low level of achievement that leaves them lacking in proficiencies for the twenty-first century (Levine in press). Third, I seriously question the social ethics and value of segregating low-achieving students into homogeneous classrooms when we know how devastating this can be to their self-concept and to their chances for subsequent education and employment (Jones in press; Oakes 1985).

In sum, it is argued that the reform movement might overlook students at both extremes of the academic parameters that define students at risk: disaffected youths who have failed school and dropped out, and semiskilled students who are marginally successful in terms of acquiring basic skills, but who are not equipped to think effectively and solve problems in a society oriented to information processing and "high-tech" occupations. Both types of students exist in cities and suburbs, but special attention is paid to the increasing numbers of the disconnected in inner cities who are more likely to suffer from poverty and disconnection from the full range of choices and responsibilities in our society, and especially from traditional family and school connections. Ironically, the reform movement may overlook disconnected students because their problems are so great, whereas it may overlook semiskilled students because they are successful in the minimal competencies required by low-level tracks and reform initiatives not aimed at cognitive development. We must attend to the needs of these students because the costs to themselves and society of not doing so are far too great.

SCHOOLS WITH MULTIPLE FUNCTIONS

Defining the Problems

What is done about students at risk depends in part on how the problems are defined. For students at risk who are disconnected, the first problem is not merely, or even primarily, lack of education. Rather, it is the total isolation of their lives from the traditional connections to the prescribed culture: stable family systems, religion, schools, gainful and rewarding employment, social and health care agencies, and legitimate political processes. It seems highly unlikely that any effort to educate these youths can succeed without first dealing with this isolation and alienation from society and with the poor physical and mental health associated with poverty, drugs, and sexuality that is both abusive and uninformed.

At the same time, while it has been useful to call attention to two types of students at risk who may be overlooked in the reform movement, the issues that apply to these students may apply in varying degrees to all students at risk. That is, we cannot readily distinguish who is and is not disaffected. Certainly, the violent youths in the adolescent underclass and the wealthier strata of society are disconnected in the extreme, but all students at risk are disconnected to some degree. In fact, the very term *at risk* connotes the risk of being disconnected from mainstream social and economic opportunities and political processes. Therefore, we should not try to differentiate among categories of students to provide different types of services and education based on poverty or family status. Intact families may be as dysfunctional as families with a single head of household; on the other hand, single-parent families may be highly functional.

Reconnecting and Educating Students at Risk

Instead, the fundamental support services and educational goals for students at risk academically should be defined on the basis of their needs. And the goals of schooling for students at risk should be threefold: (1) to reconnect them to the opportunities and responsibilities in America from which they have become isolated; (2) to provide the skills and knowledge they need to acquire, use, and produce information meaningfully and critically, as well as to solve real problems related to their lives and society's goals; and (3) to teach them to become independent learners as well as learners in collaborative contexts.

Defining the goals of schooling for students at risk in terms of reconnecting *and* educating as separate but related functions has important implications for policies and practices relating to curriculum and instruction. It is not within the scope of this chapter to consider all of these, but the following provisions are outstanding:

- *regarding the curriculum*: more meaningful learning in basic skills and the content areas, focusing on higher-order objectives, critical and creative thinking, learning how to learn, problem solving, and conceptual change; greater access to well-written literature, text-books, and instructional materials; new guidelines and curricula for areas such as parent effectiveness training for teenage parents, misconceptions in mathematics and science, comprehension monitoring, collaborative learning and problem solving, decision making, intergroup relations and governance, health care, developing a repertoire of cognitive strategies and organizational patterns, and cognitive approaches to learning a second language (e.g., Chamot and O'Malley 1987).
- *regarding instruction:* more instructional strategies formulated to involve students in the learning processes, to link new information to prior knowledge, to represent and organize new information in oral language and in prose, to transfer and apply what is learned to new areas, and to use what is learned to solve problems.
- *regarding assessment*: new tests for higher-order thinking, for use of specific thinking/learning strategies and organizational patterns, and for potential to learn. Many of the educational problems that exist today, especially for students at risk, are the result of using

standardized tests that focus on multiple choice formats and the recall of isolated facts.

- *regarding building and classroom organization*: more effort to integrate low-achieving students physically within the life of the school among students with differing talents and capabilities, rather than isolating them in tracks, rigid ability groups, and pullout programs. Strategies for doing this might include grouping for different purposes (e.g., Alvermann in press), cooperative learning in heterogeneous classrooms, flexible scheduling, group work involving intensive participation and interaction (Cohen 1986), peer tutoring and cross-age tutoring, smaller class sizes, and the use of instructional strategies such as brainstorming and discussion designed to share information.
- *regarding Chapter 1 services*: more use of funds for schoolwide instructional services and programs available to all students who need them, regardless of their family status, race, ethnic origin, or socioeconomic class; less use of pullout programs that focus on basic skills and recall of isolated facts; better coordination and accountability for students in remaining pullout programs.
- *regarding other support services*: better access to more support services to address issues of physical and mental health, poverty, family living, employment, and housing. These support services could be provided by better coordination of available services from the city and state or by inclusion of such services with school campuses. In either case, they should become part of the curriculum and instruction options for students at risk.
- *regarding dropping out*: more emphasis on prevention in terms of providing meaningful school experiences and more opportunities for "second chances" within schools. As it stands now, second-chance education is often left to interventions in private schools or within the school system in reentry centers and alternative schools, which are somehow disconnected from the heart of schooling. While such measures may be highly functional in the absence of other options, one could conceptualize schools as offering such a variety of services and programs that dropouts and adult illiterates could be educated without being isolated from the mainstream of school life.

EXISTING REFORM AGENDAS: BARRIERS AND DESIGNS FOR CHANGE

Barriers to Excellence

There is much in the new wave of reform agendas to support the vision of schooling sketched above. One of the earliest reform agendas focusing directly on students at risk came from the National Coalition of Advocates for Students (1985), which identified major causes of alienation and poor performance. According to this report, barriers to excellence begin with the various forms of discrimination that constitute both differential treatment in social and legal matters and differential access to educational, economic, and political opportunities. Barriers in school include inflexibility of school structure, abuses of tracking and ability grouping, misuses of testing, narrowness of curriculum and teaching practices, limits of vocational education, lack of support services for youth, lack of early childhood programs, and lack of democratic governance. Additionally, Parnell (1986) argues that the academic and vocational desert of American education is the high school general education program because learning then is not focused as it is in college-bound programs and vocational education programs.

Designs and Guidelines for Sustained Fundamental Change

At the time that the Advocates for Students' report was written in 1985, there were virtually no reform agendas that addressed those barriers. Now there is increasing recognition that the entire educational system is broken, not to be repaired through piecemeal efforts and quick fixes. Today there is an abundance of important reform models and guidelines that do address these barriers directly, calling for sustained fundamental changes in schools. Some of these are national reports, such as the Carnegie Foundation's (1988) special report which states:

America must confront, with urgency, the crisis in urban schools. Bold aggressive action is needed now to avoid leaving a huge and growing segment of the nation's youth civically unprepared and economically unempowered. This nation must see the urban crisis for what it is: a major failure of social policy, a piecemeal approach to a problem that requires a unified response. (p. xv)

Based on this analysis, the report defines four priorities that address the problems of urban schools:

- to affirm that every student can succeed
- to build an effective governance arrangement
- to introduce at every school a comprehensive program of renewal
- to create a network of support beyond the school.

Within this framework, the report discusses the importance of a core curriculum that has both coherence and connections to real-life experiences and the opportunity for flexible arrangements, including the concept of a Transition School that would allow students more time and options for work and study outside the walls of the school. Indeed, it is

84

encouraging to learn about the number of plans offering flexible time and work options, often educating selected youth on community college campuses, as well as involving parents and businesses directly in schools. Examples of plans described in this report include the Middle College High School in Queens (New York), in which high school students are educated on a college campus; Cincinnati's Occupational Work Adjustment Program, which allows students individualized instruction, counseling, and income from work coordinated by the school; and the national Cities-in-Schools project, which provides good counseling and help with jobs, health, and family problems.

Additionally, there are some fascinating proposals and plans for specific schools and school systems that call for sustained fundamental changes.* One of the most promising programs is provided by the Corporate/Community Schools of America (1988), which, among other things, closely coordinates health, social, and family services offered by the city to meet the needs of students without their going through as many layers of bureaucracy and delay as is normally the case. Additionally, educational, business, community, and union leaders work together to promote change. This plan, while entirely supported by business contributions, is devised to function on the budget normally allotted to public schools and is devoted to working with urban schools to incorporate its principles.

The Ohio Reading Recovery Program also has achieved dramatic successes and is being adopted in several states (see the National Diffusion Network Newsletter 1988; Pinnell et al. 1987). This program targets the poorest readers in the class for one-to-one planned lessons for 30 minutes each day. Each lesson includes reading many "little" books and compositions. Reading and writing instruction is approached holistically and is designed to teach children strategies for decoding and comprehension monitoring. Each child participates in the program until he or she has developed strategies for independent learning. Then the strategy is discontinued, and another child enters the program.

Finally, I would like to mention the recent movement for accelerated learning promoted by Levin (1987a, 1987b) and others (e.g., Cooper in press; Levine in press; Slavin 1987). For example, Calfee's (1988)

*See descriptions of specific school projects throughout the Carnegie Foundation (1988) report. See also specific school reports such as those by Dayton Public Schools (1988), which will establish an alternative school and a middle college arrangement for overage high school students, and by Cincinnati Public Schools (1988), which will begin an alternative schools program for potential dropouts with highly innovative, theme-based curricula for the ninth and tenth grades. For additional summaries and descriptions of innovative dropout prevention programs, see Fennimore (in press) and the Urban Superintendents Network report (1987). For national networks and models for restructuring schools, see the February issue of *Educational Leadership* (1988) and the National Education Association's *Visions of School Renewal* (1987), which contains numerous principles for change as well as several samples of flexible scheduling.

proposal for schools for the year 2000 focuses directly on effective curriculum and instruction, and espouses many of the values outlined above in the conceptualization of schooling for students at risk. Calfee and his colleagues envision a major national network of schools to implement a cohesive model of critical literacy, an interactive learning environment for the classroom, the school as the center of continuing inquiry, and stronger linkages among school, home, and community resources.

In general, common themes seem to connect many of the new reforms. They typically call for sustained and fundamental changes to reconnect students to the world of work and the broader community and to provide more meaningful education. Most of them also call for more flexible scheduling, individualized instruction, and low student-teacher ratios, especially for the rich array of highly innovative dropout programs and dropout prevention programs. There is also very strong support for decentralizing schools in order to reduce the size of large urban districts and to provide school-based management with parental involvement and sometimes with parental or community control over school budgets and the hiring of principals. Thus, in important ways, these reform initiatives are asking schools to become microcommunities in which the school serves as the hub of the community, with many of the services typically provided by families and other agencies to be provided through schools or physically within them. At the very least, these proposals no longer see the purpose of schools for students at risk as merely providing an education. Instead, they define schools in terms of multiple functions to educate and reconnect students to the heart of society.

Legislative and Financial Support

Interestingly, massive national and state legislation supports the reform focus on improving instructional programs for students at risk and incorporates many of the initiatives discussed above. New Chapter 1 legislation, for example, states that schools that do not show substantial progress in helping students at risk must work with local education agencies (LEAs) to modify their instructional programs. If this locally developed plan does not yield significant progress, then the LEA must work with the state education agency (SEA), the school, and the parents to formulate a joint plan of action to improve the instructional program. Additionally, Technical Assistance Centers for Chapter 1, initially authorized for assistance in program evaluation, are now authorized to serve as change agents. Specifically, they are to assist schools with program improvement, including identifying alternative curricula and effective instructional strategies—activities formerly forbidden by law! And there is provision for staff development as well as a new Specialty

Option on Curriculum and Instruction. (For a good, concise description comparing the legislation contained in House Rule 5 to the old law, see the special supplement to *Education Daily* 1988.)

This legislation is supported strongly by the Council of Chief State School Officers' recent policy titled "Assuring Educational Success for Students at Risk," which was unanimously endorsed by the Council. This policy specifies that state laws should provide the supporting health, social welfare, employment, housing, safety, transportation, and other human services which, together with the educational programs, are reasonably calculated to enable all persons to graduate from high school. This statement was further backed by a paper expressing the personal commitment of individual chief state officers to radical reform in elementary and secondary schools. Specifically, they referred to possible "state takeovers" of financially "distressed" school districts, support for student transfers from low-achieving schools or districts to "successful" locations elsewhere, and widespread utilization of knowledge gained from effective schools and effective teaching research as well as reduction in the concentration of low-achieving students at low-achieving schools (in Levine in press; see also Council of Chief State School Officers 1987).

Along with this support from national and state legislation for reform, private foundations and the business community have made significant contributions. The Casey Foundation, for example, recently gave $10-million grants to six schools that would provide some matching funds to design schools of the future, and the Carnegie Foundation's (1988) special report discusses numerous other examples. Moreover, articles abound in business journals, such as the *Harvard Business Review*, and in national newspapers describing the recent involvement of business in supporting education.

Limitations of Existing Initiatives

These reports demonstrate courage, reflection, and insight, and will undoubtedly decrease dropout rates while increasing attendance, academic achievement, and college attendance for many at-risk students. However, these reports have limitations—sometimes in what they say, and sometimes in what they omit. A major concern is the focus on basic skills, rather than on developing critical literacy, numeracy oriented to problem solving, creative thinking, and conceptual change. Similarly, there seems to be little realization of the dysfunctions of instructional practices associated with a curriculum of basic skills in regular classrooms and pullout programs such as mentioning, boring drill and practice, questions focused on isolated recall of facts, fragmented learning and instruction, dependence on unsupervised seatwork, and exercises that have no meaning (Allington in press; Ascher 1987; Peterson 1987). Equally important, this emphasis on basic skills seems to be based largely on assumptions drawn from effective schools and effective teaching research that need to be revisited in the light of recent research on expert teaching and cognitive science (see below).

Another set of problems in these current reform proposals relates to the role of building and classroom organization. On the one hand, there is some effort in a few reports to see tracking as a barrier to achievement. There is also a widespread emphasis on the need for flexible scheduling, particularly in high schools. On the other hand, many reports do not refer to the problems of segregation and poor-quality instruction that arise from tracking, ability grouping, and pullout programs for low-achieving students (e.g., Peterson 1987). It is imperative that the reform movement relate to the increasing body of literature showing that such arrangements typically produce differential access to educational opportunities in terms of instructional materials and instructional strategies (Allington in press; Ascher 1987; Good and Marshall 1984; Peterson 1987). That is, high-ability students consistently receive more active instruction, more comprehension instruction, and more opportunities for comprehension monitoring. In contrast, teachers of low-achieving students tend to assume that these students cannot attain higher-order objectives and consequently provide mainly drill and practice, decoding, and algorithms for rote memorization (see Jones in press; National Coalition of Advocates for Students 1985; National Education Association 1987; Oakes 1985; Salmons 1988; Slavin 1986). These problems are compounded by the lack of coordination between Chapter 1 instruction and that of the regular classroom, leading to fragmentation of learning and instruction and to lack of accountability for student programs (Allington in press; Ascher 1987; Gartner and Lipsky 1987; Peterson 1987).

While it is exciting to hear about reforms for school-based management, they could be implemented in ways that are just as disastrous as centralized structures for governance and administration are. Specifically, there is a high potential that the parents and community members who sit on advisory councils will not be informed about curriculum and instruction, and will have heavily vested interests in basic skills, drill and practice, and the recall of isolated facts. Some may even believe that efforts to teach thinking are a form of brainwashing. More important, some degree of centralization in the area of curriculum and instruction at the elementary grades may be needed to assure continuity of instruction for the highly mobile students in urban schools. It is interesting to note, for example, that while most school systems are moving toward school-based management, Detroit moved toward more centralization when community/parent-based administrative layers were removed (Michigan Public School Act, no. 71, April 14, 1982). However, parent involvement continues to remain high at the school level.

Additionally, there seems to be little reference to the need for different kinds of tests. It is axiomatic that tests drive instruction, and many of the recommended reforms will require massive changes in testing to assess higher-order thinking as well as students' learning potential and thinking/learning strategies. In assessing learning potential, it is not students' past experience that counts; rather, it is their ability to respond to instruction. One measure of this is the Learning Potential and Assessment Device developed by Feuerstein and his colleagues (Feuerstein et al. 1985). Learning strategy tests assess students' knowledge and their use of specific learning strategies (for a discussion of the Learning and Study Skills Inventory developed by Weinstein and her colleagues, see Weinstein and Underwood 1985). However, much more research needs to be done to develop a diversity of measures for all grade levels and for assessment of conceptual understanding in the content areas. We also need more training for teachers and publishers so they can develop tests for use in the classroom that focus on higher-order thinking (see Arter and Salmon 1987; Stiggins, Rubel, and Quellmalz 1986).

Finally, concerns about staffing were expressed during a recent planning meeting in Chicago on restructuring schools, sponsored by the North Central Regional Educational Laboratory. Both teachers and administrators were worried about the recruitment of minority teachers, evidence of increasing preferences for white teachers not to teach minority students, the commitment and quality of instruction among those teachers and administrators nearing retirement, and the lack of understanding generally of the characteristics of different types of at-risk students.

To summarize, the reform movement has identified numerous barriers to excellence and equity, and has proposed a rich array of designs for tomorrow's schools, focusing on governance structures, scheduling, parent/community relations, more meaningful curriculum, and more effective instructional strategies. Moreover, there is substantial support from national, state, and local legislators for new reforms as well as increasing support in the business community.

Concerns about the reform movement center on widespread assumptions about curriculum and instruction. Specifically, it is argued that basic skills instruction, pullout programs, ability grouping, and tracking are barriers to effective instruction for low-achieving students. Moreover, in the light of recent research, we must reevaluate models of effective schools and effective teaching, as well as who teaches thinking and what is taught.

DIMENSIONS OF CHANGE

Support for reforms for students at risk marks a major turning point for American education. But we must take care that this new wave of reform focuses directly on changes in curriculum and instruction for low-achieving students. We must also build the foundation for these changes on valid models of effective learning, teaching, and instructional leadership. In the final analysis, schools and their governance structures are essentially shells or frameworks within which curriculum and instruction, the heart of schooling, take place. As we remodel our notion of schooling, so, too, must we remodel our concepts of learning, teaching, and leadership that will carry out the ultimate intent of the reforms for these students. We must keep in mind constantly the goals of the reform movement—namely, reconnection to the larger society, cognitive development, and empowerment to live and work in society peacefully and collaboratively.

Vision of Learning

Traditional Models

The current emphasis on teaching isolated basic skills through extended periods of drill and practice can be traced back to behaviorism as a focus of psychology (Resnick 1987). Specifically, behaviorists argued that learning occurred through repeated associations between a stimulus and a response. Research indicated that learning was more effective when practice and feedback were distributed or spaced over different periods of time. Additionally, behaviorists assumed that an individual's cognitive capacity to process information was limited to approximately seven discrete items; therefore, instruction should be presented in small chunks and steps. Thus, the learner was conceptualized as a passive person on whom information was essentially imposed by repeated associations. According to this view, all the learner had to do was decode the words (because somehow the meaning was "in" the words) and be exposed to various associations between stimuli and their appropriate responses.

Recent Models of Learning

It would be impossible to review here the deluge of research emerging from cognitive psychology, as well as research on specific subjects that challenges the behaviorist point of view. This research, which began in the early 1970s, has essentially stood behaviorism on its head by emphasizing the importance of what happens in the brain between the stimulus and the response. Today's vision of learning conceptualizes the model learner as someone working actively to construct meaning, to plan strategically, to monitor comprehension and problem solving, to integrate new information with prior knowledge, and to apply and use what is learned. In this vision, comprehension is defined as an interaction among the reader, the text, and the context, and memory is conceptualized as a network of knowledge structures that relate information in many dimensions or attributes. Learning occurs as the learner calls upon a repertoire of cognitive and metacognitive strategies to represent and integrate the new information and to link it to these networks.*

Cognitive psychologists recognize that there are differences in aptitude among high- and low-achieving students. However, they consistently support teaching at-risk students a repertoire of cognitive and metacognitive strategies such as problem solving, representation, elaboration, summarizing, clarifying, using graphic organizers and organizational patterns, comprehension monitoring, self-questioning, verbal self-instruction and self-regulation, hypothesis generation, and study skills (Jones, Tinzmann et al. 1987; Palincsar and Brown 1985; Peterson 1987; Schoenfeld 1988; Singer and Donlan 1982; Weinstein and Mayer 1986). In fact, they argue that training in generalizable cognitive strategies has more powerful and longer-lasting effects than does teaching discrete cognitive skills (Bransford et al. 1986; Corno and Snow 1986). This is particularly true for students at risk. However, there is substantial evidence in this same literature that students at risk may *not* apply these strategies spontaneously without sustained, explicit strategy instruction.

An example of such a strategy is one that my colleagues and I now refer to as S2ROS: (1) *Survey* the text, looking for specific types of text structures; (2) *Represent* the structure (organizational pattern) in a mental picture or graphic; (3) *Read* to refine or modify the mental representation, clarify what is unclear, and monitor comprehension; (4) *Outline* the text using graphic organizers that reflect the text structure; and (5) *Summarize* the outline, using the graphic organizer to structure the summary (for a description of these procedures, see Jones, Pierce, and Hunter in press). In this strategy, the learner uses various graphic outlines to help represent, outline, and summarize the information. Organizational patterns used in this strategy include theme and supporting statements; compare and contrast; sequence of events, including stages in a life cycle; and problem and solution (Jones, Tinzmann et al. 1987; see also Jones, Pierce, and Hunter in press). What follows is an example of a model learner applying this strategy to a history text:

---

*In reading, see Anderson et al. (1985); Jones, Palincsar et al. (1987); Paris, Lipson, and Wixson (1983); Pearson and Johnson (1978); and Tierney, Readence, and Dishner (1988). In mathematics, see Linquist (in press); Schoenfeld (1985, 1988); Silver (1985); and *Educational Psychologist* (1988). In science, see Anderson and Smith (1987); and Carey (1986).

He reads the section title: *Why Did the English Come to the New World?*... "Hmmm, there must be reasons why the Englishmen came to the new world." His finger moves to the first subtitle, which he reads: *America Offered the Chance to Make a Better Living.* "There's a reason why they came to the new world." His finger then moves to the second subtitle: *America Offered Freedom of Worship.* "That's also a reason why they came to the new world." His finger moves to the third subtitle.... He looks up to reflect. "So from here I can make a spider map." He draws an imaginary spider map with a central node on the pages of his textbook. *"Why did the English come to the new world?* goes in the middle, the central node of the map. *Freedom of worship, better living, and possibility of sharing in government* go on the other sides." He draws three imaginary legs of the spider map.

He looks at the questions at the end of the section.... *(2) What were some of the important reasons that brought English settlers to the new world?* "Well, I just read three or four reasons that brought English settlers to the new world." *(3) What was a trading company?* "Well, I don't know what a trading company was; I have to read to find out that answer." *(4) How were the trading companies...?* "Hmmm, trading companies again...the trading companies must be important because they ask two questions about them."

He turns to the second section of the chapter, placing his finger on the section title: *How Did Virginia Become the First Successful English Colony?* "How...when I see the word 'how,' I think of events." His finger moves to the first subtitle: *Sir Walter Raleigh's Attempt to Start a Colony Fails.* "That's an event." He pauses, with a brief glance back to the title, then to the subtitle. "But [the subtitle] said [the colony] failed, but [the title] said it became the first successful English colony. That's strange." He begins to skim the paragraph below the subtitle. "I see North Carolina. [Walter Raleigh] must have failed in North Carolina before he became successful in Virginia." His finger moves to the second subtitle: *English Settle in Jamestown....* "That's an event on how Virginia became the first successful English colony." *Jamestown Settlers Encountered Difficulties.* He looks up to reflect. "So, they must have had problems before the colony became successful. Over here there's a map." He scans the map briefly with his finger, saying, "Pennsylvania. Here's Virginia and Jamestown. Jamestown is a city of Virginia. Here's North Carolina, the state under Virginia." He pauses a moment, then places his finger on the third subtitle for this section....

I have focused on this example for two reasons: (1) it demonstrates the complexity of skilled learning and the learner's coordination of cognitive and metacognitive strategies, and (2) the student who demonstrated the "think aloud" strategy for a video teleconference is the same student described previously as Harlow (Jones et al. 1988). Interestingly, members of the audience commented that we should not have picked such a skilled learner to demonstrate strategies for the average student! Unfortunately, while Harlow can apply this strategy comfortably to various texts and has commented repeatedly on how easy it is, whether or not he actually uses this strategy will depend on the tests he is given. If he continues to be tested only for recall of isolated facts, he probably will not use the strategy. It will also depend on whether or not his teachers encourage him to use it—which leads to the question of defining roles for effective teaching.

Effective Teaching

Traditional Models

Clearly, it is not within the scope of this chapter to review the various models for effective teaching. However, one widely used model from that strand of research is illustrative. In 1983, Rosenshine (1983) defined the teaching functions from effective classrooms in an award-winning article (see also Rosenshine 1986). These functions include the following: review prior learning, present material in small steps with explanations and active student practice after each step, provide for understanding, provide systematic feedback and testing, and so on.

Although all of these functions are important, this model and others like it omit many of the values and strategies associated with expert teaching and cognitive instruction. That is, the functions above do not provide for anchoring the instruction in functional contexts (e.g., Bransford et al. 1986; Stitch and Hickey in press), effectively teaching students to become strategic learners (e.g., Paris, Lipson, and Wixson 1983), or teaching for conceptual change (Anderson and Smith 1987).

For example, cognitive psychologists such as Winograd and Hare (in press) define explicit instruction very differently from the notion of direct instruction implied in various effective teaching models. In the latter, direct or explicit instruction means that the teacher presents a skill *as an end in itself* and explains how to use it with guided practice and comprehension monitoring. In contrast, explicit instruction from the perspective of cognitive psychologists means that the teacher presents the skill *as a means to learning the content*, models the application of specific thinking strategies, explains why they are important and when to use them, *and* provides extensive coaching for transfer that goes far beyond guided practice with feedback. In this version, the focus is on teaching students to be strategic learners, and the instruction is anchored in content instruction and use.

There is another problem with the effective teaching model. Its thrust toward teacher-directed instruction is antithetical to recent literature on collaborative learning (e.g., *Educational Leadership* 1987) that advocates teaching students to become independent learners who are capable of evaluating their own learning (Palincsar 1987), and indeed encourages reforms for critical literacy. In a biting criticism of the effective teaching model, Wise characterizes it as leading to an "educational world" in which "passive learners" are "fed basic skills in bit-sized chunks to be regurgitated on command before the next scrap of spartan fare can be served," and in which there is a lack of concern for such themes as "individualism, individual freedom, creativity, analytical thinking, and international competitiveness of the twenty-first century" (Levine in press).

Renewed Models of Effective Teaching

In a recent analysis of the research on effective teaching, Brophy (1988) argues that since most of the effective teaching research has been conducted with students in classrooms using Chapter 1 funding, the model is appropriate for students at risk. He also acknowledges, however, that it needs to be extended to include the teaching of cognitive and metacognitive strategies. While these modifications are vital, and Brophy is to be commended for identifying this need for adaptation, they do not fully address the criticisms above (see Jones and Friedman 1988).

Moreover, there is a flourishing literature on expert teaching and cognitive instruction to guide reform. Some of these visions of teaching and schooling are general but would benefit students at risk especially. Shulman's (1987) model, for example, emphasizes comprehension and reasoning, transformation, and reflection, and provides a useful portrait of an expert teacher. In Reigeluth's (1987) model of schooling, teachers are guides who orchestrate the resources of schools, parents, and community as well as of richly stocked learning labs and cluster schools. I would also refer the reader to the articles on collegial learning in *Educational Leadership* (1987), as well as to Collins, Brown, and Newman (in press) for a discussion of the principles of instruction involved in the most successful instructional interventions from cognitive psychology.

Other principles of learning and instruction from cognitive psychology address students at risk specifically. Jenkins, Pious, and Peterson (in press) have examined effective and ineffective instruction for learning-disabled students and for educable mentally retarded students in different categories. They argue that the most successful instruction in these categories is more similar than different and question the value of separate instruction.

Additionally, Brown, Palincsar, and Purcell (1986) have written an excellent article entitled "Poor Readers: Teach, Don't Label" in which they argue that poor readers have become poor readers largely by being successful in the substandard fare of basic skills instruction offered to them in most schools. They call for integrating instruction for students at risk into the regular classroom, provided that it is academically rich and that the teacher offers effective cognitive instruction. Reciprocal teaching is an example of a cognitive instruction developed by Palincsar and Brown (1985) for low-achieving students. This approach teaches students four strategies—self-questioning, clarifying, summarizing, and predicting—in the context of a dialogue between the teacher and students during which the teacher gradually transfers responsibility for learning to the students. Other examples of cognitive instruction appropriate for students at risk may be found in works related to the concept of strategic teaching (see Jones, Palincsar et al. 1987; Jones, Tinzmann et al. 1987; Palincsar et al. 1986).

Models of reform for students at risk should take into consideration the differences in models from expert teaching and cognitive instruction, as distinct from traditional models of effective teaching. However, it is hoped that future models of effective teaching will incorporate more fully the research from expert teaching and cognitive instruction, so that effective teaching will be closer to the meaning of expert teaching.

Instructional Leadership and Effective Schools

Traditional Visions

The May 1988 issue of *Education and Urban Society* focuses on the reform theme "Rethinking School Leadership." Several articles feature analyses of instructional leadership. To my dismay, all of them drew their definitions and frames of reference from the literature on leadership, school culture and organization, and the sociology of the classroom. Certainly all of these topics are important for effective school functioning. However, not one of the authors typically writes about curriculum and instruction, and in the entire issue, there were almost no references to research on expert teaching, staff development, curriculum and instruction, or instruction in any of the content areas! This tendency to define instructional leadership exclusively in terms of leadership rather than instruction is not limited to this one publication; rather, it runs throughout the literature on instructional leadership.

There is an equivalent lack of focus on curriculum and instruction in the literature on effective schools. In general, this literature still focuses largely on strong leadership, high expectations for students, accountability for teachers, monitoring of student progress, teaching of skills to all students, and clarity of curriculum objectives. All of these factors are indeed vital to establishing an effective school, to be sure. Nevertheless, it is questionable whether principals, superintendents, and other instructional leaders can make appropriate decisions about curriculum, instruction, and grouping, when so much of the literature they read does not address these problems directly and in depth.

Renewed Visions

Happily, some effective school researchers do focus on the changes in curriculum and instruction needed for students at risk. Pink and Liebert

(1986), for example, discuss the inadequacies of school leadership for instruction, of basals in general, and of instruction for students at risk, as well as other barriers to effective instruction. Among other things, they recommend (1) developing district reading objectives based on an analysis of students' needs and reasons for student failure, rather than on the content of the basals; (2) aligning the basal text to these objectives, (3) extending reading instruction for low-achieving students to focus on reading for meaning and reading to learn instead of on learning isolated subskills, and (4) providing staff development for teachers and building leadership that focuses on issues of curriculum and instruction.

Stedman (1988) argues that the list of correlates for effective schools should be amended to provide (1) academically rich programs that stress cognitive development, not just basic skills; (2) attention to goals involving cultural pluralism and multicultural education; (3) cooperation between educators and parents; and (4) emphasis on solving students' personal problems and developing their social skills.

Levine and his colleagues (Levine this volume and in press; Levine and Cooper in press) have written excellent discussions relating explicit comprehension instruction, strategic teaching, and the characteristics of effective comprehension instruction for low-achieving students to the effective schools movement and the process of school change. They also discuss the need for better models of teacher education as vital links in the change process. Clearly, we must apply all that we know about learning and teaching to improve models of teacher education.

Finally, Sizer (in Brandt 1988) discusses what is probably one of the most serious problems of curriculum and instruction for all students, and especially for low-achieving students: the sheer amount of information that students are expected to learn (Peterson 1987). It is outrageous and highly destructive to the learning process for students to have textbooks with 500–700 pages of facts and details with no guidelines as to how to select, sequence, or prioritize; with few summaries, questions, or highlights of key information; and with little emphasis on strategies to help students understand key concepts and applications of what they read (Tyson-Bernstein 1988). Sizer argues that it is vital in this wave of reform to establish what is essential to teach and for what purposes, and to have instructional leaders committed to implementing such reforms.

Changes in Who Teaches Thinking

Who teaches thinking? The answer to this question determines to a great extent *how* thinking will be taught. If it is taught in a skills course, objectives for skills and strategies will drive the sequencing of instruction. If it is taught in the context of a content course, content

96

objectives will drive the sequencing of instruction. There is considerable debate as to which context is more effective for teaching at-risk students. On the one hand, Feuerstein and his colleagues (Feuerstein et al. 1985) argue that low-achieving students may experience cognitive overload if they must learn both content and skills simultaneously. Accordingly, they have developed *Instrumental Enrichment* as an adjunct program, using content-free geometric shapes and pictures. Most other adjunct programs for teaching thinking, however, use a combination of prose and visual formats. On the other hand, others argue that instruction should be content driven because a substantial part of skills and strategies is content specific and because it typically does not transfer easily to other areas (Resnick 1987).

In a sense, both arguments are true. Thus, the position taken here is that content-driven skills instruction, in which skills are learned as a means to learning the content or solving problems, is generally preferable, unless students are having great difficulty with the content. In this event, additional strategy instruction might be very helpful, provided that transfer is built into the instruction and that the substance of the adjunct program is well coordinated with the content courses.

What Skills and Strategies Are Taught

To some extent this issue has already been discussed. However, the importance of moving students at risk from "LOTS" (low-order thinking skills) to "HOTS" (higher-order thinking skills) cannot be overemphasized. We can no longer continue to assign high-achieving students to a HOTS curriculum and low-achieving students to a LOTS curriculum on grounds of equity or quality of instruction. All too often, teaching basic skills means teaching low-achieving students many fragmented skills in contexts that are boring and demoralizing, while high-achieving students in the next room are enjoying a challenging curriculum and sustained instruction focusing on essential skills for critical thinking and problem solving. To put it simply, low-achieving students are unlikely to become productive citizens if they are never given the same opportunities to participate that high-achieving students are.

We must be careful as to what skills are taught, however. According to Feuerstein and his colleagues (Feuerstein et al. in press), many of the programs for higher-order thinking are not appropriate for low-achieving students because these students may need prerequisite instruction. At the same time, there seem to be some core thinking skills that are research based and apply across a variety of content areas, although there may be varying definitions as to what these would be. For example, Marzano and his colleagues (Marzano et al. 1988) have identified 21 core skills that would be appropriate for schools that are teaching essential skills, rather than a hierarchy of skills and subskills (compare Jones, Tinzmann et al. 1987). But there may be considerable variation in defining such skills and implementing them systematically in the curriculum.

A final issue in considering what is taught is the notion that while some subject areas such as mathematics are clearly hierarchical in nature, there is little evidence to suggest that younger students and low-achieving students must learn low-order skills before learning higher-order ones in the language arts. There is ample evidence, however, that primary students can learn to summarize, clarify, question themselves, and regulate their learning processes in important ways (e.g., Palincsar and Brown 1985). This is not to say that it is easy to teach them; to the contrary, as stated above, they need sustained instruction. Rather, the intent here is to challenge the widespread practice of teaching skills in each course of study according to a lock-step sequence based on a taxonomy, regardless of the context.

In closing, it is important to emphasize again that there is substantial funding available for schooling from public resources, private foundations, and businesses, and these monies are likely to increase in future years. The budget for Chapter 1 is now $3.9 billion, the federal government's largest investment in education, and there is language in this budget to apply it for alternative curricula, schoolwide instruction programs, and better coordination of Chapter 1 programs with the regular classroom. Moreover, many of the funds from businesses, private foundations, and states allow for coordinating and integrating many support services to schools to address the social, physical, and economic needs of students at risk. If ever there was a time to experiment and reform, to enact one's hopes for future generations, to be pioneers and models for years to come, it is now.

DISCUSSION QUESTIONS

1. How has the population of at-risk students changed since studies were made of disadvantaged youths in the 1960s, and what effects are these changes likely to have on American society?

2. What are the characteristics of skilled learning behavior, and how do these differ from the fragmented, short-term responses often made by at-risk students?

3. What does the learning model presented in the example above teach the student (Harlow) about metacognitive activity during his studying?

4. If teachers actually use strategic instruction with at-risk students, what assumed practices may they need to change?

REFERENCES

Allington, R. L. In press. How policy and regulation influence instruction for at-risk learners; Why poor readers rarely comprehend well and probably never will. In *Dimensions of thinking and cognitive instruction,* ed. B. F. Jones and L. Idol. Hillsdale, N.J.: Lawrence Erlbaum Associates.

Alvermann, D. E. In press. Strategic teaching in social studies. In *Strategic teaching and learning: Cognitive instruction in the content areas,* ed. B. F. Jones, A. S. Palincsar, D. S. Ogle, and E. G. Carr. Alexandria, Va.: Association for Supervision and Curriculum Development.

Anderson, C. W., and Smith, L. 1987. Teaching science. In *The educator's handbook: A research perspective,* ed. V. Koehler, 84–110. New York: Longman.

Anderson, R. C.; Hiebert, E. H.; Scott, J. A.; and Wilkinson, I. A. G. 1985. *Becoming a nation of readers: The report of the Commission on Reading.* Urbana: University of Illinois.

Arter, J. A., and Salmon, J. R. 1987. *Assessing higher order thinking skills: A consumer's guide.* Technical Report. Portland, Oreg.: Northwest Regional Educational Laboratory.

Ascher, C. 1987. *Chapter 1 programs: New guides from the research.* New York: Columbia University, Teachers College, ERIC Clearinghouse on Urban Education.

Brandt, R. 1987. On changing secondary schools: A conversation with Ted Sizer. *Educational Leadership* 45(3): 30–36.

Bransford, J. D.; Sherwood, R.; Vye, N.; and Rieser, J. 1986. Teaching thinking and problem solving. *American Psychologist* 41:1078–89.

Brophy, J. 1988. Research linking teacher behavior to student achievement: Potential implications for instruction of Chapter 1 students. *Educational Psychologist* 23:235–86.

Brown, A. L.; Palincsar, A. S.; and Purcell, L. 1986. Poor readers: Teach, don't label. In *The school achievement of minority children: New perspectives,* ed. U. Neisser, 105–43. Hillsdale, N.J.: Lawrence Erlbaum Associates.

Calfee, R. 1988. Schools for the year 2000: A proposal and planning document for fundamental change in American schools. Unpublished document available from the author at Stanford University.

Carey, S. 1986. Cognitive science and science education. *American Psychologist* 41:1123–30.

Carnegie Foundation for the Advancement of Teaching. 1988. *An imperiled generation: Saving urban schools.* Special Report. Princeton, N.J.: the Foundation.

Chamot, A. U., and O'Malley, J. M. 1987. The cognitive academic language learning approach: A bridge to the mainstream. *TESOL Quarterly* 21:227–49.

Cincinnati Public Schools. 1988. *Cincinnati high school of excellence.* Cincinnati, Ohio: Cincinnati Public Schools.

Cohen, E. 1986. *Designing groupwork: Strategies for the heterogeneous classroom*. New York: Teachers College Press.

Collins, A. M.; Brown, J. S.; and Newman, S. In press. Cognitive apprenticeship: Teaching students the craft of reading, writing, and mathematics. In *Knowing and learning: Issues in a cognitive science of instruction*, ed. L. B. Resnick. Hillsdale, N.J.: Lawrence Erlbaum Associates.

Cooper, E. J. In press. Toward a mainstream of instruction for American schools. *Journal of Negro Education*.

Corno, L., and Snow, R. E. 1986. Adapting teaching to individual differences among learners. In *Handbook of research on teaching*. 3d ed., ed. M. C. Wittrock, 605–29. New York: Macmillan.

Corporate/Community Schools of America. 1988. Corporate/community schools of America: Progress report. Unpublished manuscript available from Primus Mootry, Better Boys Foundation, 407 South Dearborn, Suite 600, Chicago, IL 60605 (312–427–0468).

Council of Chief State School Officers. 1987. Assuring educational success for students at risk. Paper published by the Council, Washington, D.C.

Dayton Public Schools. 1988. *University Prep Program (Prep)*. Dayton, Ohio: Dayton Public Schools.

Education and Urban Society. 1988, May. Special issue: Rethinking school leadership.

Education Daily. 1988, June. Special supplement: Education programs reauthorized through 1993.

Educational Leadership. 1987, November. Special issue: Collegial learning.

Educational Leadership. 1988, February. Special issue: Restructuring schools to match a changing society.

Educational Psychologist. 1988, Spring. Special issue: Learning mathematics from instruction.

Fennimore, T. In press. *A guide for dropout prevention: Creating an integrated learning environment in secondary schools*. Columbus, Ohio: National Center for Research on Vocational Education.

Feuerstein, R.; Jensen, M. R.; Hoffman, M. B.; and Rand, Y. 1985. Instrumental enrichment, an intervention program for structural cognitive modifiability: Theory and practice. In *Thinking and learning skills*. Vol. 1, *Relating instruction to research*, ed. J. W. Segal, S. F. Chipman, and R. Glaser, 43–82. Hillsdale, N.J.: Lawrence Erlbaum Associates.

Feuerstein, R.; Rand, Y.; Hoffman, M. B.; Epozi, M.; and Kaiwel, S. In press. Intervention programs for the retarded performer: Goals, means, and expected outcomes. In *Dimensions of thinking and cognitive instruction*, ed. B. F. Jones and L. Idol. Hillsdale, N.J.: Lawrence Erlbaum Associates.

Gartner, A., and Lipsky, D. K. 1987. Beyond special education: Toward a quality system for all students. *Harvard Educational Review* 57:367–95.

Good, T. L., and Marshall, S. 1984. Do students learn more in heterogeneous or homogeneous groups? In *The social context of intuition: Group organization and processes*, ed. P. L. Peterson, L. C. Wilkinson, and M. Halliman. New York: Academic Press.

Jenkins, J.; Pious, C. G.; and Peterson, D. L. In press. Categorical programs for remedial and handicapped students: Issues of validity. *Exceptional Children*.

Jones, B. F. In press. Text learning strategy instruction: Guidelines from theory to practice. In *Learning and study strategy research: Issues in assessment, instruction and evaluation,* ed. E. Goetz, P. Alexander, and C. E. Weinstein. New York: Academic Press.

Jones, B. F., and Friedman, L. B. 1988. Active instruction for students: Remarks on merging process-outcome and cognitive perspectives. *Educational Psychologist* 23:299–308.

Jones, B. F.; Palincsar, A. S.; Ogle, D. S.; and Carr, E. G., eds. 1987. *Strategic teaching and learning: Cognitive instruction in the content areas.* Alexandria, Va.: Association for Supervision and Curriculum Development.

Jones, B. F.; Palincsar, A. S.; Ogle, D. S.; Carr, E. G.; Walker, B. J.; and Hixson, J., producers. 1988. *Strategies for teaching reading as thinking.* Detroit: Public Broadcasting Service and North Central Regional Educational Laboratory. Video teleconference.

Jones, B. F.; Pierce, J.; and Hunter, B. In press. Using graphic representations for analysis and problem solving. *Educational Leadership.*

Jones, B. F.; Tinzmann, M.; Friedman, L. B.; and Walker, B. J. 1987. *Teaching thinking skills: English/Language Arts.* Washington, D.C.: National Education Association.

Lamar, J. V. 1988. Kids who sell crack. *Time,* 9 May, 20–33.

Levin, H. M. 1987a. Accelerated schools for disadvantaged students. *Educational Leadership* 44(6): 19–21.

Levin, H. M. 1987b. New schools for the disadvantaged. Paper prepared for the Mid-Continent Regional Educational Laboratory, Denver.

Levin, J. R. 1976. What have we learned about maximizing what children learn? In *Cognitive learning in children: Theories and strategies,* ed. J. R. Levin and V. L. Allen, 105–34. New York: Academic Press.

Levine, D. U. In press. School effectiveness and reform. In *Introduction to the frontiers of education,* ed. A. O. Ornstein and D. U. Levine. Boston: Houghton Mifflin.

Levine, D. U., and Cooper, E. J. In press. The change process and its implications in teaching thinking. In *Dimensions of thinking and cognitive instruction,* ed. B. F. Jones and L. Idol. Hillsdale, N.J.: Lawrence Erlbaum Associates.

Linquist, M. In press. Strategic teaching and learning in mathematics. In *Strategic teaching and learning: Cognitive instruction in the content areas,* ed. B. F. Jones, A. S. Palincsar, D. S. Ogle, and E. G. Carr. Alexandria, Va.: Association for Supervision and Curriculum Development.

Marzano, R. J.; Brandt, R.; Hughes, C.; Jones, B. F.; Presseisen, B.; Rankin, S.; and Suhor, C. 1988. *Dimensions of thinking: A framework for curriculum and instruction.* Alexandria, Va.: Association for Supervision and Curriculum Development.

National Coalition of Advocates for Students. 1985. *Barriers to excellence: Our children at risk.* Boston: the Coalition.

National Diffusion Network Newsletter. 1988. *Reading recovery* 2 (February).

National Education Association. 1987. *Visions of school renewal.* Washington, D.C.: the Association.

Neisser, U., ed. 1986. *The school achievement of minority children: New perspectives.* Hillsdale, N.J.: Lawrence Erlbaum Associates.

Newsweek. 1988. Black and white: How integrated is America? 7 March, 18–43.

Oakes, J. 1985. *Keeping track: How schools structure inequality*. New Haven, Conn.: Yale University Press.

Palincsar, A. S. 1987. Collaborating for collaborative learning of text comprehension. Paper presented at the annual meeting of the American Educational Research Association, Washington, D.C.

Palincsar, A. S., and Brown, A. L. 1985. Reciprocal teaching: Activities to promote "reading with your mind." In *Reading, thinking, and concept development: Strategies for the classroom*, ed. T. L. Harris and E. J. Cooper, 147–60. New York: College Entrance Examination Board.

Palincsar, A. S.; Ogle, D. C.; Jones, B. F.; and Carr, E. D. 1986. *Teaching reading as thinking*. Facilitators Manual. Alexandria, Va.: Association for Supervision and Curriculum Development.

Paris, S. G.; Lipson, M. Y.; and Wixson, K. 1983. Becoming a strategic reader. *Contemporary Educational Psychology* 8:293–316.

Parnell, D. 1986. *The neglected majority*. Washington, D.C.: Community College Press.

Pearson, P. D., and Johnson, D. C. 1978. *Teaching reading comprehension*. New York: Holt, Rinehart & Winston.

Peterson, P. 1987. Selecting students and services for compensatory education: Lessons from aptitude-treatment interaction research. In *Designs for compensatory education: Conference proceedings and papers*, ed. B. I. Williams, P. A. Richmond, and B. J. Mason. Washington, D.C.: Research and Evaluation Associates.

Pink, W. T., and Liebert, R. E. 1986. Reading instruction in elementary schools: A proposal for reform. *Elementary School Journal* 87:51–67.

Pinnell, G.; Lyons, C.; Young, P.; and Deford, D. 1987. *The reading recovery project in Columbus, Ohio: Volume VI, Year 2, 1986–87*. Technical Report. Columbus: The Ohio State University.

Reigeluth, C. M. 1987. Search for meaningful reform: A third-wave educational system. *Journal of Instructional Development* 10:3–14.

Resnick, L. B. 1987. *Education and learning to think*. Washington, D.C.: National Academy Press.

Rohwer, W. D., Jr. 1971. Prime time for education: Early childhood or adolescence? *Harvard Educational Review* 41:316–41.

Rosenshine, B. 1983. Teaching functions in instructional programs. *Elementary School Journal* 83:335–51.

Rosenshine, B. 1986. Synthesis of research on explicit teaching. *Educational Leadership* 43:60–69.

Salmons, S. 1988. The tracking controversy. *New York Times Education Life*, 10 April, 56ff.

Schoenfeld, A. H. 1985. *Mathematical problem solving*. New York: Academic Press.

Schoenfeld, A. H., ed. 1988. *Cognitive science and mathematics education*. Hillsdale, N.J.: Lawrence Erlbaum Associates.

Schorr, L. B., and Schorr, D. 1988. *Within our reach: Breaking the cycle of disadvantage*. New York: Anchor Press.

Shulman, L. S. 1987. Knowledge and teaching: Foundations of the new reform. *Harvard Educational Review* 57(1): 1–22.

Silver, E. A., ed. 1985. *Teaching and learning mathematical problem solving.* Hillsdale, N.J.: Lawrence Erlbaum Associates.

Singer, H., and Donlan, D. 1982. Active comprehension: Problem-solving schema with question generation for comprehension of complex short stories. *Reading Research Quarterly* 17:166–86.

Slavin, R. E. 1986. *Ability grouping and student achievement in elementary schools: A best-evidence synthesis.* Report no. 1. Baltimore, Md.: The Johns Hopkins University, Center for Research on Elementary and Middle Schools.

Slavin, R. E. 1987. Cooperative learning and the cooperative school. *Educational Leadership* 45(3): 7–13.

Stedman, L. 1988. The effective schools formula still needs changing. *Phi Delta Kappan* 69:439–42.

Stiggins, R. L.; Rubel, E.; and Quellmalz, E. 1986. *Measuring thinking skills in the classroom.* Washington, D.C.: National Education Association.

Stitch, T. G., and Hickey, D. T. In press. Functional context theory, literacy, and electronics training. In *Instruction: Theoretical and applied perspectives,* ed. R. Dillon and J. Pellegrino. New York: Praeger Press.

Tierney, R. J.; Readence, J. E.; and Dishner, E. K. 1988. *Reading strategies and practices—A compendium.* 2d ed. Boston: Allyn & Bacon.

Tyson-Bernstein, H. 1988. *A conspiracy of good intentions: America's textbook fiasco.* Washington, D.C.: Council for Basic Education.

Urban Superintendents Network. 1987. *Dealing with dropouts.* Washington, D.C.: Office of Educational Research and Improvement, U.S. Department of Education.

Weinstein, C. E., and Mayer, R. E. 1986. The teaching of learning strategies. In *Handbook of research on teaching.* 3d ed., ed. M. C. Wittrock, 315–27. New York: Macmillan.

Weinstein, C. E., and Underwood, V. L. 1985. Learning strategies: The how of learning. In *Thinking and learning skills.* Vol. 1, *Relating instruction to research,* ed. J. W. Segal, S. F. Chipman, and R. Glaser, 241–58. Hillsdale, N.J.: Lawrence Erlbaum Associates.

Winograd, P. N., and Hare, V. C. In press. Direct instruction of reading comprehension strategies: The nature of teacher explanation. In *Learning and study strategy research: Issues in assessment, instruction, and evaluation,* ed. E. Goetz, P. Alexander, and C. Weinstein. New York: Academic Press.

6. INTELLECTUAL ASSESSMENT OF AT-RISK STUDENTS: CLASSIFICATION VS. INSTRUCTIONAL GOALS*

by Trevor E. Sewell

Should the outcome of psychological services in the schools be judged by the scientific and technical properties of the assessment instruments used? Or, rather, should psychological services be evaluated by the quality of the instructional outcome achieved for children? From whatever perspective one examines the controversy over testing in America's schools, a central issue is the key role played by IQ in determining special class placement. If one assumes that the central purpose of testing is selection and classification, then scientific support for the IQ test is indeed impressive, although also controversial. But if the quality of educational programming becomes the conceptual basis for testing, then the psychometric tradition is brought into conflict with the practical need to link testing to instructional goals. In the education of at-risk students, this conflict is central to understanding the role assessment can play in both instruction and curricular planning.

The following facsimile letter was sent from the Superintendent of Schools in a hypothetical urban school district to the Director of Special Education Services in that same district:

Dear Dr. Jane Doe:

Thank you for the excellent report on the status of special education in the district. You have done a commendable job in providing detailed information on the type of children we serve and the nature of the services provided to these children and their families. Your report, however, has generated the following concerns:

First, the disproportionate overrepresentation of ethnic minority children in the mildly educable classes is alarming. Can this factor be accounted for by the existence of a high percentage of at-risk or economically disadvantaged children in the district, the assessment procedures, or merely a continuation of traditional professional practices in special education?

*I wish to express profound appreciation to Calvin F. Nodine and Vivian D. Price for their thoughtful comments on this chapter.

104

Second, is it unreasonable that I should be deeply concerned with the glaring underrepresentation of ethnic minority students in the classes for gifted and talented students?

Finally, the report, although documenting impressively the services provided for the mildly educable mentally retarded children in self-contained classes, has not included any evaluation data on the effectiveness of these programs.

In light of these observations, there seem to be compelling reasons to raise critical questions about our assessment procedures, the effectiveness of the services provided mildly retarded students, and, more importantly, the extent to which assessment and diagnostic information are linked to the instructional needs of children.

I would greatly appreciate your sharing your thinking on these issues with me at your earliest convenience.

Yours sincerely,

John Q. Leader
Superintendent of Schools

I will not respond specifically to the superintendent's concerns. However, the issues I will raise in this chapter regarding the assessment of at-risk children, and especially minority children, are deeply embedded in the concerns noted in his letter. My objective is to discuss assessment from the practical perspective of the needed intervention for children who are at risk of academic failure. The concerns raised by the superintendent are much more than the abstract scientific issues being debated by academic psychologists. They are the central political and legal issues in our society which are intertwined with the social problems of restricted educational opportunities.

The recognized cultural gap between socioeconomic classes is perhaps the primary causal factor to which low academic test scores are attributed. Thus, there is a widely held position that performance on standardized tests—largely requiring acquired knowledge—is invariably influenced by cultural and educational exposure. If one subscribes to the hypothesis that culturally loaded tests are biased against those whose experiential background is appreciably different from that of middle-class children, then the evidence of cultural distinctiveness among many low test performers is pervasive.

Most academic psychologists are intimately aware of the favorable conditions under which the majority of America's children are reared. They know of the level of physical, social, and psychological care

105

provided, and they know of the quality of the cognitive stimulation associated with middle-class child-rearing practices. They know of the emotional investment of parents in transmitting culturally important elements of the dominant society, and they know, too, of the care with which experiences or stimuli are selected, filtered, and presented to children.

There is, however, another social reality faced by those to whom we refer as at risk. These children live in a world in which although biological dysfunction may be absent, the dehumanizing nature of the social conditions will frequently result in differential risk for impaired cognitive development, if corrective intervention is not undertaken. The recognition of this adverse social reality is implicit in the question raised by Scarr (1981b): "How many more disadvantaged children would have been bright if they had had middle-class gestation and rearing conditions?" (p. 68).

Professional psychologists and educators tend to contrast the physical environments of advantaged and disadvantaged children, and conclude that the cognitive performance of the poor can be logically explained by such a disparity. Given the known connections among cognitive performance, health, nutrition, and family socioeconomic status (Birch and Gussow 1970), this line of reasoning seems to be based on sound empirical evidence. But shouldn't the subtle impact of the sociopolitical system also be factored into this causal explanation? Ginsburg (1986) and Ogbu (1978) have alerted us to the consequences of the behavior and belief systems associated with class and caste status. From this perspective it is reasonable to ask, To what extent is the motivation to learn or to perform on tests shaped by the implicit belief that socioeconomic rewards are predetermined by one's race or place in the social system? To what degree are learning outcomes influenced by teacher expectations (Rosenthal and Jacobson 1964), as well as by school policies that are linked to social class, ideological position, and occupational stratification? Given the evidence that poverty is not an insurmountable obstacle to high academic achievement for those who are disadvantaged in a social sense (Edmonds 1986), perhaps we need to reconceptualize performance expectations in order to nullify our own self-fulfilling prophecy.

Over fifteen years ago in a perceptive, yet cynical observation, Stein (1971) identified strategies for failure that are quite relevant today as society apparently retreats from basic standards of fairness for minorities. Citing the high rate of functional illiteracy among students in Black and Puerto Rican schools after eight years of schooling, she posed a provocative question: Could this extraordinary record of failure be attributed primarily to "professional" educators? Stein explicitly argued that the responsibility for unacceptable levels of failure must be shared with the business community, city politicians, the courts, housing authorities, and the medical community which provided active support for persistent failure. This line of reasoning provides the context in which we can examine the policies by which many educational systems over past decades have met a perceived goal of reproducing the labor force. Perhaps inadvertently, schools have perpetuated a differential pattern of social class achievement by supporting curriculum and administrative structures designed to ensure that the nation's need for professionals, as well as for low-status workers, will be met by the existing social and ethnic stratification found in the labor market. There is a striking paradox, however, in the public's perception of who should be blamed for the failure of our schools to meet the needs of society. Although business leaders are the most persistent critics of American education's poor products, many do not see themselves as having any responsibility for helping to correct the schools' problems. The chairman of the Xerox Corporation forcefully articulated this view in a message to 1988 presidential candidates. Without citing business as sharing any responsibility for the academic outcomes of schools, he denounced education as a failed monopoly that produces workers with "a 50 percent defect rate" (*New York Times* 1987).

Although much of the controversy and many of the legal battles that center around testing focus largely on cultural bias factors, the emotional arguments generated from the theoretical perspective that tests measure immutably fixed, innate intellectual capacity must be critically scrutinized relative to the practice of teaching intellectual skills.

Whatever constitutes intelligence includes thinking skills. Stated from another perspective, effective thinking bears a close relationship to what is referred to as intellectual competence (Sternberg 1987). Thus, the underlying psychological theory of the nature of intelligence is a critical issue, particularly with respect to Blacks who constitute a large percentage of the at-risk population.

It is most encouraging that psychologists and educators who advocate intellectual-skills training programs are *not* taking their cues from what standard IQ tests measure. Rather, they have found the notion of fixed, innate abilities conceptually incompatible with their objective of teaching critical and creative thinking to all youngsters (Feuerstein 1980). What remains to be conclusively demonstrated to critics of this position, however, is evidence the intellectual competence of at-risk children can actually be raised (Reynolds 1987).

When viewed in a historical context, this criticism suggests that arguments supporting the cultural bias hypothesis in assessment have not been convincing and that forces advocating biological determinism in intellectual competence are still alive and well in American psychology. However, the instructional methods derived from this point of view

107

are not well formulated. Biological determinism, which has been unresponsive to reason, logic, and data, is an ideological force that reinforces and perpetuates ineffective educational practices for at-risk children who are in need of creative assessment and intervention strategies.

In spite of the adverse educational consequences associated with IQ testing, and the legal victories in which charges of cultural bias were not refuted by the defendants (e.g., *Larry P. v. Wilson Riles* 1979), empirical data based on psychometric and statistical analysis have provided formidable support for the validity of IQ testing (Jensen 1980). The enormous body of data amassed to support the technical properties of IQ tests and the assertion that such tests are not significantly biased have not helped to defuse the criticism that these tests have questionable educational benefit in assessing children's intellect. We should note that even when an IQ test is viewed as unbiased with respect to a certain class of criteria, it is widely believed that the question of bias is formulated and defined too narrowly (Sternberg 1987; Scheuneman 1987). But even if we assume, for the sake of practice, that an IQ test is unbiased, there is doubt as to whether the evidence of instructional benefits exists (Heller, Holtzman, and Messick 1982).

Should, then, the outcome of psychological services in the schools be judged by the scientific and technical properties of the assessment instruments used? Or, rather, should psychological services be evaluated by the quality of the instructional outcome achieved for children? Let us examine these questions.

TESTING FOR INSTRUCTIONAL OUTCOME

From whatever perspective one examines the controversy over testing in America's schools, a central issue is the key role played by IQ in determining special class placement. This psychometric measure is rooted in Binet's (Binet and Simon 1916) conception of a test design to sort, rank, and classify children who could not profit from regular class instruction. Within this practical framework, the full weight of scientific psychology supports the IQ test.

If one assumes that the central purpose of testing is selection and classification, then scientific support for the IQ test is indeed impressive, although controversial. The technical adequacy of the IQ test for predicting academic achievement justifies the contention that the test is valid for all subgroups of the population (Cleary et al. 1975; Jensen 1980). But if the quality of educational programming becomes the conceptual basis for testing, or if the search for more effective instructional methods is a key reason for testing, then the psychometric

108

tradition is brought into conflict with the practical need to link testing to instructional goals (Sewell 1979, 1987). The psychometric goal does not deal with a major focus of the IQ critics, which is the social policy consequences of testing; nor does it "provide the kinds of information about process that seems to be necessary for an effective training program that seeks, in fact, to train students in the process (or products) of learning" (Wagner and Sternberg 1984, p. 193).

Although measurement technology has improved substantially over the past fifty years, psychologists have largely failed to focus on the distinction between tests designed for understanding the processes involved in learning and those used to rank or classify individuals on the basis of educational products.

If the accountability demanded by today's educational reform movement should be extended to testing practices, we need to raise a number of measurement issues in reference to achievement outcomes. Most central is the concern over the issue of *instructional validity* as a technical feature concerned with the assessment benefits to children. Why hasn't this issue been raised more frequently in psychometric methodology? Also, should one interpret the information derived from the psychometric instruments designed for the specific goal of selection and classification as implying instructional relevance as well? The answer is No because of the fundamental distinction between product and process goals. The distinction between testing for classification, in which questions of validity and test bias have generated a stream of controversy, and assessing in order to enhance instructional outcomes must be recognized.

One observer of the outcome of the psychometric approach (Elliott 1987) has pointed out that a low score on a college admissions test will mean one will not be selected to attend the college of his or her choice. Similarly, a low score on an employment test will mean the applicant will not be hired or the employee will not be promoted. However, a low score on an IQ test usually means the student will be selected for special education placement. If the purpose of testing in schools is reconceptualized so "testing and teaching become integral events," as Glaser (1985) suggests, pedagogical concerns should dictate that low scores on assessment instruments lead to differential instructional strategies. Instructional decisions should be based on intraindividual performance. Low scores should facilitate and inform instructional actions, thus effectively linking assessment information to the educational needs of the particular child.

EDUCATIONAL IMPLICATIONS OF THE USE OF IQ DATA

Whether one interprets the history of IQ testing as "one of psychology's greatest achievements" (Herrnstein 1973) or as "one of its most shameful moments'' (Kamin 1974; Scarr 1981a), there is a growing suspicion that IQ testing of poor and minority children simply perpetuates social myths and restricts access to educational opportunities. Nevertheless, support for the perspective that IQ testing is indeed a laudable accomplishment rests partially on the questionable perception that ''Testing on a broad scale was adopted by the schools to improve the opportunities of lower-SES and minority children for selection into educationally and occupationally advantaged positions and to reduce the pervasive class and ethnic bias of personal judgment'' (Scarr 1981b, p. 4).

In a balanced presentation centered around the use of IQ tests, Travers (1982) highlighted the proponents' position that IQ tests offer the best chance for individuals of disadvantaged background to achieve competitive advantage in occupational selection. In line with this position, the subjective and qualitative assessments associated with teachers' ratings have been persistently depicted as potentially more discriminatory than the test. This line of reasoning presents a rather striking conceptual confusion because of the failure of psychologists to differentiate between testing for instructional purposes and testing to determine eligibility for occupational selection or special class placement. Moreover, when the educational use of an IQ test is viewed within the historical context, it is difficult to defend the position that it was widely adopted in the interest of lower-SES and minority children.

To the contrary, we find substantial evidence that IQ tests have been used to *restrict* the educational opportunities of minority children. The narrow technical sense in which testing issues are analyzed has not always taken into account the issue of fairness or the implications of the impact of ideological views on institutional practices. For example, when launching the prestigious Stanford-Binet Intelligence Test, Terman (1916) stated that all Blacks, Spanish-Indians, and Mexicans should be segregated into special classes because they could not master abstraction.

In the 1980s, if minorities are still being victimized by the degradation inherent in segregation, massive and persistent unemployment, pervasive and increasing violations of civil rights, and social isolation, isn't it indeed amazing and inconceivable that in the early 1900s, with his insight and conceptual ability to contribute so profoundly to psychometric theory and development, Terman lacked the insight to realize that sociocultural factors significantly influence test performance? It seems reasonably clear that the obvious and fundamental reason for this line of test interpretation was that prevailing psychological theories relative to minorities blended harmoniously with the demands of the social order. Psychologists used the IQ as ''scientific'' support for a narrow definition of educability, which historically has effectively excluded minorities (Snow 1982). Thus, the educational practices of

110

tracking, segregation, and special class placement have been deeply embedded in the very foundations of the testing movement.

The social and political realities for minorities have radically shifted from the exclusionary educational policies of the past to an increasing emphasis on equity. Consequently, our current educational use of tests needs to be grounded in sound professional practices conceptualized to remediate cognitive and educational deficiencies. Fortunately, an increasingly influential group of cognitive psychologists and educators (Feuerstein 1980; Sternberg 1987) has been motivated by their views of intellectual competence to participate actively in shaping educational policy and curricula by promoting thinking-skills training programs for many at-risk student groups.

TEACHING THINKING SKILLS

The consequence of a growing interest in teaching thinking has been the development of a diverse set of pre-establishment cognitive programs geared to a wide range of age and ability groups. Also reflected in this diversity of programs is a cognitive framework in which the program goals are developed. Whether one argues that a goal of teaching thinking should be to remedy particular deficiencies in cognition (Baron and Sternberg 1987) or to frame the program in a broader concept of "cognitive modifiability," which refers to the expectation of structural changes facilitated by program intervention (Feuerstein 1980), the implicit assumption is that higher-level problem-solving skills are required for educational success. Thus, for at-risk children who are especially vulnerable to developmental problems in cognitive functioning, the teaching of thinking fits a primary educational goal for enhancing students' intellectual development in school.

To this end, a cognitive skills training program (Sewell et al. 1984) with a special focus on educable mentally retarded (EMR) children was undertaken in an urban school district. In describing this program, we focus on the institutional intrigues of *implementing* a cognitive skills program, rather than on its general results. The cognitive skills program was advocated and implemented to focus attention on low-intellectual-aptitude students with the intent of achieving the following objectives: (1) to encourage administrators and teachers to act toward these students in curriculum planning as if the students were capable of developing higher levels of problem-solving skills; (2) to expose children systematically to a thinking-skills program that could be integrated into the school's regular curriculum; and (3) to determine the effect of the curriculum-based thinking-skills program in facilitating cognitive skills development and academic achievement—both process and product.

Perhaps educators might recommend a thinking-skills program because of its emphasis on broad, well-articulated goals such as "making students better all-round thinkers" (Sternberg 1987) or as "a prerequisite for good citizenship" (Nickerson 1987). In this instance, however, the low cognitive and academic performance of students in EMR classes presented a compelling reason to solicit support for a particular kind of thinking-skills program. We should note that the professional decision alone of placing mildly retarded children in self-contained special education classes—based on the rationale that available special resources, specialized curricula, and individualized teaching strategies would produce educational benefits—was not productive. And, in fact, efficacy studies have *not* supported the assumption that special instructional programs alone produce beneficial effects for the mildly retarded (Glass 1985; Carlberg and Kavale 1980).

If the effectiveness of special education has not been demonstrated, then the adequacy of the instructional program must be brought into sharp focus. Based on traditional practice, one can also argue that diagnostic and placement decisions occur independently of evaluation data about the quality of instruction to which the child has been exposed in regular classrooms. Since academic performance plays a pivotal role in the process of referral and classification for EMR placement, an evaluation of the adequacy of the learning opportunities in regular education for disadvantaged and minority children should be required prior to placement decisions. Systematic instructional intervention, whether in special or regular education, is necessary for at-risk children. The teaching of thinking skills is perhaps a defensible mechanism to provide instructional intervention in either setting.

In the study described, the teachers of five special education classes volunteered to implement the program. Six all-day training sessions were held for these teachers. The training focused on two goals: (1) to introduce the theoretical principles underlying the thinking-skills training program, and (2) to emphasize the importance of transfer to the regular school curriculum in the teaching of the program.

The teachers' enthusiasm for the program was the most powerful force found in the implementation process. Teachers convinced parents and school administrators not only that the program was in the best interest of a small group of children, but also that its availability in the classroom projected the view that the school was receptive to innovative instructional strategies and that the school's approach to EMR children implied these youngsters are capable of higher levels of cognitive functioning.

Perhaps the combination of teacher enthusiasm and parental involvement generated the unparalleled level of student motivation. The opportunity for these school-certified EMR students to demonstrate the instruments of the thinking-skills program to students in regular classrooms further strengthened their motivation to improve their overall levels of adaptive functioning. Furthermore, when a parent made a highly unusual visit to the school to share her enthusiasm and support for the program—support derived from seeing her child engaged in a homework assignment—and was told by her child in an appropriate context, "Mom, please *restrain your impulsivity*" (a concept used in the training program), the image of special education began shifting from school specific to adaptable to everyday life. Cognitive skills as measured by intelligence tests showed significant improvement over the course of a year. However, improvement on standardized achievement tests was not in line with predictions. It is noteworthy that during the intervention phase, two of the EMR children were decertified by interdisciplinary teams. But despite the pressing demand for the program by the teachers, and despite the measured progress by students, the program failed to receive support at the state level under which the project was initially funded. This decision not to support the program was made prior to review of the evaluation data. Does this mean factors that are most influential in shaping professional practices in the schools are powerfully linked to ideological convictions and are not necessarily based on merits of the debates regarding technical or scientific issues in education and psychology?

Returning to the exemplary letter to Jane Doe, the response of the Director of Special Education Services to the Superintendent could be based on several of the key points raised in this discussion.

Dear Superintendent Leader:

First, although the number of children classified as EMR has declined significantly in contrast to those of other categories of handicapped children in this district, there is an overrepresentation of minority children due to the following factors.

- A large number of minority children perform poorly in academic subjects, a factor that usually triggers the referral process. Evidently the performance of these children in regular education is a matter that should be given critical attention.
- The IQ test still plays a key role in the placement decision in this district, despite a growing sensitivity to the impact of cultural experience on children's test performance.
- Although judicial opinions are in conflict as to the nature of cultural bias in IQ tests, massive evidence indicates that IQ scores are highly related to family circumstances, educational experience, and a general cultural gap in the socioeconomic

113

status of the students. Given the low-income background of a large percentage of at-risk students in this district—particularly minority students—whether learning ability can be accurately inferred from the IQ scores is questionable. Consequently, district staff are currently evaluating other assessment procedures that minimize past learning experiences in the assessment process. They are also looking into more dynamic test designs.

Second, the conceptual linkage between testing and instructional methods is clearly established historically, theoretically, and empirically. In reality, however, the traditional emphasis on IQ usage is primarily *on predicting* future school success rather than on providing instructional guidance. The shift in focus to an approach in which assessment is geared to inform instruction is gaining considerable attention and merits further examination.

Third, the underlying assumptions governing special educational practices suggest that the district's instructional methods should be effective. Empirical support for these assumptions is limited. The district findings on the effectiveness of special education programs agree with the national data. The trend is toward increasing emphasis on innovative programs such as thinking-skills training programs and other instructional strategies that focus on the wide range of individual differences in the mildly retarded category.

Our commitment to the effective education of every child generates the necessity for continuous experimentation with innovative and creative approaches to educating the mildly mentally handicapped child. To this end, we have instituted thinking-skills training programs and explored opportunities to use alternative assessment procedures, especially with poor and minority children. And, most importantly, the district must actively seek to eradicate any educational practice that implicitly or explicitly contributes to a lack of equity in instructional opportunities. The youngsters in America's schools deserve our concentrated attention to this end.

Sincerely,

Dr. Jane Doe
Director of Special Education Services

DISCUSSION QUESTIONS

1. How might the use of intelligence tests negatively influence teachers' views of student performance?

2. Tracking, placement, and labeling might be outcomes of the ill use of standardized testing. What are some other outcomes of testing, and upon what principles should such tests be constructed?

3. Some thinking skills programs have been implemented with at-risk populations. Although clear findings on student change are not available, what seems to be the overall response of teachers who have used the materials?

4. What implications does the concept of cognitive modifiability have for the administrative structure and district policies followed in the area of special education?

REFERENCES

Baron, J. B., and Sternberg, R. J., eds. 1987. *Teaching thinking skills: Theory and practice.* New York: W. H. Freeman.

Binet, A., and Simon, T. S. 1916. *The development of intelligence in children.* Baltimore, Md.: Williams & Wilkins.

Birch, H., and Gussow, J. 1970. *Disadvantaged children: Health, nutrition and school failure.* New York: Harcourt, Brace & World, Inc.

Carlberg, C., and Kavale, K. 1980. The efficacy of special versus regular class placement for exceptional children: A meta-analysis. *Journal of Special Education* 14:295–309.

Cleary, T.; Humphreys, L.; Kenrick, S.; and Wesman, A. 1975. Educational uses of tests with disadvantaged students. *American Psychologist* 30:15–41.

Edmonds, R. 1986. Characteristics of effective schools. In *The school achievement of minority children: New perspectives,* ed. U. Neisser, 93–104. Hillsdale, N.J.: Lawrence Erlbaum Associates.

Elliott, R. 1987. *Litigating intelligence: IQ tests, special education, and social science in the courtroom.* Dover, Mass.: Auburn House.

Feuerstein, R. 1980. *Instrumental enrichment: An intervention program for cognitive modifiability.* In collaboration with Y. Rand, M. B. Hoffman, and R. Miller. Baltimore, Md.: University Park Press.

Ginsburg, H. P. 1986. The myth of the deprived child: New thoughts on poor children. In *The school achievement of minority children: New perspectives,* ed. U. Neisser. Hillsdale, N.J.: Lawrence Erlbaum Associates.

Glaser, R. 1985. The integration of instruction and testing. Paper presented at the ETS Invitational Conference on the Redesign of Testing for the 21st Century, Princeton, N.J.

Glass, G. 1985. Effectiveness of special education. *Policy Studies Review* 2:65–78.

Heller, K.; Holtzman, W.; and Messick, S., eds. 1982. *Placing children in special education: A strategy for equity.* Washington, D.C.: National Academy Press.

Herrnstein, R. 1973. *IQ in the meritocracy.* Boston: Little, Brown.

Jensen, A. 1980. *Bias in mental testing.* New York: Free Press.

Kamin, L. 1974. *The science and politics of IQ*. Potomac, Md.: Lawrence Erlbaum Associates.

Larry P. v. Wilson Riles. 1979. N.CO–71–2270 RFP, U.S. District Court for Northern District of California.

New York Times. Schools let down U.S., Xerox chairman says. October 27, 1987.

Nickerson, R. 1987. Why teach thinking? In *Teaching thinking skills: Theory and practice*, ed. J. Baron and R. Sternberg. New York: W. H. Freeman.

Ogbu, J. 1978. *Minority education and caste: The American system in cross-cultural perspective*. New York: Academic Press.

Reynolds, C. 1987. Raising intelligence: Clever Hans, Candide, and the miracle in Milwaukee. *Journal of School Psychology* 25:309–12.

Rosenthal, R., and Jacobson, L. 1964. Teacher expectations for the disadvantaged. *Scientific American* 218:19–23.

Scarr, S. 1981a. Testing for children: Assessment and the many determinants of intellectual competence. *American Psychologist* 36:1159–66.

Scarr, S. 1981b. Dilemmas in assessment of disadvantaged children. In *Psychological influences in retarded performances*, ed. M. Begab, H. C. Haywood, and H. Garber. Baltimore, Md.: University Park Press.

Scheuneman, J. 1987. An argument opposing Jensen on test bias: The psychological aspect. In *Arthur Jensen*, ed. S. Modgil and C. Modgil. New York: Falmer Press.

Sewell, T. 1979. Intelligence and learning tasks as predictors of scholastic achievement in Black and white first grade children. *Journal of School Psychology* 17:325–32.

Sewell, T. 1987. Dynamic assessment as a nondiscriminatory procedure. In *Dynamic Assessment*, ed. C. Lidz. New York: Guilford Publications.

Sewell, T.; Winikur, D.; Berlinghof, M.; Berkowitz, C.; and Miner, M. 1984. Cognitive modifiability of retarded performers. Paper presented at the Annual Conference of the National Association of School Psychologists, Philadelphia.

Snow, R. E. 1982. The training of intellectual aptitude. In *How and how much can intelligence be increased*, ed. D. K. Detterman and R. J. Sternberg. Norwood, N.J.: Ablex Publishing.

Stein, A. 1971. Strategies for failure. *Harvard Educational Review* 41:158–204.

Sternberg, R. 1987. Gee, there's more than *g*! A critique of Arthur Jensen's view on intelligence. In *Arthur Jensen*, ed. S. Modgil and C. Modgil. New York: Falmer Press.

Terman, L. 1916. *The measurement of intelligence*. Boston: Houghton Mifflin.

Travers, J. 1982. Testing in educational placement: Issues and evidence. In *Placing children in special education: A strategy for equity*, ed. K. Heller, W. Holtzman, and S. Messick. Washington, D.C.: National Academy Press.

Wagner, R., and Sternberg, R. 1984. Alternative conceptions of intelligence and their implications for education. *Review of Educational Research* 54:179–223.

7. TEACHING THINKING TO AT-RISK STUDENTS: GENERALIZATIONS AND SPECULATION

by Daniel U. Levine

After providing a general definition that identifies at-risk students as those whose poor performance hinders subsequent success and frequently leads to withdrawal from the educational system, this chapter offers several generalizations regarding teaching thinking skills to these students. Matters of instruction, mediation, motivation, process change, program development, and comprehensive approaches are discussed. Following a series of speculations on topics such as bilingual education, learning-style instruction, structure change, and program support, the chapter concludes with an enumeration of the most prominent pitfalls and obstacles likely to impede the improvement of thinking instruction for at-risk learners.

Since there is no accepted definition of *at-risk students*, one can define this term however one likes. In general, I will use it to refer to low-achieving students whose poor performance hinders subsequent success and frequently leads to withdrawal from the educational system.

I originally expected that the task of reviewing and making sense of the already large and rapidly growing body of literature on teaching thinking in general and its implications for at-risk students in particular would prove to be somewhat overwhelming. Like you, I constantly come across many journal articles and numerous references to new books dealing with instruction to improve students' thinking. For a nonspecialist unable to stay fully up to date with every important aspect of this emerging field, obtaining an adequate grasp of the major developments and issues presents an imposing challenge.

Happily, I found that this task was not quite as difficult as it seemed at first. Excellent books and papers that identify and discuss key developments in a comprehensible manner are now available; the newcomer need not venture out alone and unguided into impenetrable forests. Several of the most useful and important of these sources will be cited in the following pages.

However, after being pleasantly surprised by the relative lucidity that now seems to characterize the literature on teaching thinking, I soon concluded that the task of actually devising and delivering effective instruction to improve the thinking and other high-order skills of at-risk students is even more overwhelming and difficult than I thought previously. I will highlight my reasons for this conclusion throughout this chapter. The first section offers some generalizations regarding instruction for at-risk students and the actions that should be taken to improve their performance with respect to higher-order skills. The second section presents and discusses several issues that should be considered speculative at the present time. The final section itemizes some of the tendencies and pitfalls that I believe are most worrisome as we work to improve thinking and other higher-order skills among low-achieving students.

GENERALIZATIONS

My first general conclusion is that *instruction for at-risk students typically places little emphasis on the development of thinking and other higher-order skills*. Instead, stress usually is put on small mechanical skills and on rote memory and regurgitation. Research support for this conclusion is substantial; for example, Porter and his colleagues (Porter et al. 1986) reviewed the research on the teaching of mathematics and reported that low-performing students "spend far more time learning facts and computational skills," while high-performing students "spend more time understanding mathematical concepts and applications" (p. 12). Of course, many observers (including Porter and his colleagues) also would say the modal instructional pattern for *most* students places little emphasis on development of thinking skills (e.g., Goodlad 1984); from this point of view, instruction for at-risk students may not be very different from that provided for average students.

Second, *improvement of at-risk students' performance with regard to thinking and other higher-order skills will require careful and continuous mediation by teachers and other adults*. This generalization is both a guiding principle and a conclusion of Brainin's (1985) assessment of the literature on approaches to improving students' cognitive functioning. After noting that the student of "particular interest" in this analysis was the "lower functioning preadolescent or adolescent" (p. 124), Brainin reviewed Feuerstein's *Instrumental Enrichment* program and several other approaches for "mediating" the development of cognitive functioning among low achievers. Brainin concluded:

> There is a substantial body of work emanating from curriculum developers, instructional, cognitive, and developmental psychologists, learning theorists, and scholars and practitioners in related disciplines which can inform a pedagogic model designed to enhance thinking abilities. Much of that work offers support to a set of essential conditions for effective mediation [that requires the mediator] to share with the learner an intentional and analytic approach to the learning process itself; to develop an awareness of the

118

meaning of stimuli and their relevance in ever-larger contexts increasingly remote from direct experience; and to enable learners to experience and express cognitive growth in productive ways. (p. 139)

The term *mediated learning*, as used by Brainin and others, postulates and implies that the teacher must provide close and specific guidance during the early stages of learning. Mediated learning thus involves strong intervention so that students are given not merely appropriate tasks and materials but also personal assistance in learning to master them. As noted by Brainin (1985), approaches that assume low-achieving students, "already discouraged by many years of past school failure, could become 'self-regulated learners' with only minimal intervention" (p. 143) are not adequate.

Several other authors stress the importance of mediated learning as a general principle in improving the thinking of all groups of students, not just previously low achievers. For example, Jones (1986) argues for a general concept of the teacher as a mediator of "students' cognitive processing" who helps students "activate prior knowledge, represent information, select specific strategies, construct meaning, monitor understanding, assess the use of a strategy, organize and relate ideas, summarize, and extend learning" (p. 9). Similarly, Marzano and his colleagues (Marzano et al. 1988) have described and advocated for a mediator who "works actively to help the learner interpret the environment [and also helps the learner in] focusing attention, [conceptualizing] strategies as means to learning, linking new information to prior knowledge, and explaining how ideas are related" (p. 236). Putnam, Roehler, and Duffy (1987) have described teachers who help improve student comprehension as those who "respond spontaneously to the restructuring of students" in the process of interacting with them, "provide differential explanations to different students," "give suitable assistance depending on the students' difficulties," and ensure that "students develop an understanding of how to use the skill in real text" (p. 3). We can logically conclude that if average students need these kinds of mediated assistance to become more competent thinkers, those who start as low achievers require even stronger and more consistent mediated intervention. Such an emphasis on mediation for low achievers has obvious implications in terms of class size, teaching load, and availability of materials for schools with many low achievers.

Brown (1985) has cited convincing evidence to support the proposition that students who are less prepared need even more help than do those who are better prepared. After concluding that educators should focus on teaching "intermediate level" thinking skills rather than a "large number of specific routines" or "some extremely general supervisory ones" (p. 331), Brown points out that "impulse-control" approaches, which have been used successfully to help average students develop thinking skills, are "insufficient for the problem learners who do not already know how to perform the task-specific elements" in solving problems. She also proceeds to describe and summarize metacognitive and related approaches that she and her colleagues—particularly Palincsar—have developed and implemented successfully to help previously low-achieving students internalize and master "comprehension-monitoring" and "comprehension-fostering" activities in the classroom (pp. 331–33). Similarly, Meichenbaum (1985) has described successful methods that he and his colleagues have developed to help "impulsive children" internalize self-management and thereby overcome deficits in cognitive functioning, in line with the theories of such cognitive scientists as Luria and Vygotsky.

Third, *the success of efforts to substantially improve the thinking skills of at-risk students will depend on other related changes such as improvements in students' motivation to learn, self-discipline, and mastery of basic skills and knowledge in diverse curriculum areas. In short, success in this endeavor requires fundamental improvement in schools and classrooms as a whole*, not just the introduction of another instructional package or approach to teach thinking.

Although scholars who have been developing or studying approaches to improve thinking use differing terminologies and perspectives when discussing these considerations for at-risk students, their importance is recognized regularly in the literature. For example, regarding the central role of *motivation* and *affective* aspects of instruction to improve thinking, Baron (1985) emphasizes the importance of the learner's values and expectations in developing "fundamental components" of intelligence, while Bruner (1985) stresses the centrality of the emotional relationship between teacher and student. As these writers point out—and as every thoughtful educator knows well—concern for motivation immediately raises many complicated, related issues involving self-concept, students' attributions of success and failure, the contributions of teacher, parental, and peer expectations and influences, and other significant matters.

Closely related to questions of motivation are the *self-discipline* and *impulse control* of at-risk students, also of major concern to many scholars in the movement to improve thinking skills. Indeed, Marzano and his colleagues (Marzano et al. 1988), Brown (1985), Scardamalia and Bereiter (1985), and many others consider self-regulation of thought processes and behavior patterns in the classroom to be a central component of competence in thinking and reasoning, particularly among low-achieving students who initially lack such capabilities. Thus, as indicated previously, the development of self-regulated thought processes and behaviors (often discussed as "control of impulsivity") has become the explicit goal of many approaches to improving students' thinking.

Regarding the importance of a *solid base of content knowledge and basic skills*, Case (1985), Weinstein and Mayer (1986), Nickerson, Perkins, and Smith (1985), and many others have stressed that students must acquire the "working memory" and relevant knowledge necessary to complete specific conceptual tasks. At the same time, Brown (1985), Jones (1986), Marzano and his colleagues (Marzano et al. 1988), and other observers emphasize the importance of developing and engaging students' prior knowledge in helping them to improve their comprehension of increasingly difficult subject material. As with motivation, impulse control, and self-regulation, development and application of prior knowledge are central concerns in many of the approaches that have been or are being developed to improve the thinking of low-achieving students. Several programs now provide instruction in heuristics or procedures that enhance students' information management.

Fourth, *the success of projects to teach thinking and other higher-order skills to low-achieving students depends on teachers' willingness and capacity to move beyond structured, passive learning and to progressively introduce more active learning experiences for students.* On the one hand, most scholars who are working to develop or assess thinking-skills projects agree that students must play a more active part in directing and regulating their own learning (e.g., Brown 1985; Good 1987; Goodlad 1984; Sizer 1984). On the other hand, low-achieving students frequently are reluctant and/or unprepared to do this (Doyle 1983), and, as emphasized above, they require much mediated assistance to become involved, active learners. In addition, teachers encounter particularly difficult management problems when they attempt to move beyond structured, passive learning in classrooms with a high proportion of low achievers; as a result, teachers tend to fixate on highly structured methods that produce order and some progress in mastery of the basic skills. Sedlak and his colleagues (Sedlak et al. 1986) have described this tendency as a "social trap" in which success in classroom management can "delude" teachers into thinking they are meeting their responsibilities" at the expense of the formal objective of maximizing academic learning" (p. 102). This situation is not helped much by the fact that many efforts to move rapidly toward active, independent learning in schools enrolling many disadvantaged students have produced little more than chaos in the classroom (Levine and Havighurst 1988).

Fortunately, some approaches to improving higher-order skills among low achievers may help teachers move beyond passive learning to the structured assistance and learning that help students become progressively more active learners. For example, Brown (1985) has described and

121

summarized several techniques that appear to help low achievers move gradually toward more active and proficient self-regulation in learning. However, I doubt whether teachers can use such techniques effectively unless strong steps are first taken to ensure that their classes are manageable. In addition, substantial staff development and other forms of appropriate assistance or teacher support must be readily available to these instructors.

These conclusions regarding the importance of manageability and assistance in helping teachers and students move beyond passive learning lead to my fifth generalization, which recognizes that *projects to improve thinking among low-achieving students must take account of research on the change process and its implications for the design and implementation of substantial innovations in education*. Cooper and I recently prepared a paper on this topic (Levine and Cooper in press); rather than review that paper in detail, I will quote from parts of the discussion and conclusions in the final section:

- Because thinking-skills approaches require relatively large, complex, and difficult changes in the behaviors and attitudes of teachers and students, even more stress than usual should be placed on ensuring that innovations are manageable and implementable for teachers, and that prerequisites and antecedents (discussed earlier in this paper) of successful implementation are firmly in place. Concern for manageability and implementability should include attention to such considerations as planning time, class size, change overload, amount of paperwork, adaptability in participating classrooms, compatibility with demands already placed on teachers, and capacity of the innovation for inspiring enthusiasm and commitment among teachers and students. Regarding staff-development requirements in helping teachers learn to deliver higher-order instruction effectively, Kurth and Stromberg (1984) have reported that the staff development required is "Herculean." Similarly, research conducted by Putnam, Roehler, and Duffy (1987) indicated that "the staff development effort must be quite elaborate when the goal is to develop cognitive understanding . . . and independent decision making" among teachers, rather than technical prescriptions (p. 24).
- Related to manageability issues and to the importance of problem identification and resolution in implementing innovations successfully, educators implementing thinking-skills projects should identify in advance the obstacles likely to impede implementation and take definite steps to overcome them. Among the obstacles that generally impede efforts to center instruction on the development of thinking and other higher-order skills are: institutional realities of schools that stress classroom order and passive learning (Goodlad, 1984); students' preferences for lower-order skills (Doyle, 1985); compromises between students and faculty who trade obedience for undemanding instruction (Sedlak, Wheeler, Pullin, and Cusick, 1986); low-level learning scripts teachers utilize with low achievers (Payne, 1984; Shavelson, 1985); teacher preferences for easy-to-teach lessons (Levine and Havighurst, 1988); and state-government mandates to stress lower-order skills (McNeil, 1986; Rosenholtz, 1987).

- Special considerations and problems regarding approaches for improving students' thinking skills suggest that successful implementation will require unusual stress on revising organizational and institutional arrangements and structures. Preceding sections of this paper cited research (e.g., Crandall, Eiseman, and Louis, 1986; Corbett and D'Amico, 1986; Miles, 1987) pointing to the importance of change in organizational procedures and arrangements in successful implementation of significant innovations. This is likely to be particularly true with respect to thinking-skills projects because they generally will require considerable cooperation and coordination across teachers and classrooms, and because there is much current uncertainty regarding the integration of subject-matter and process objectives, the sequencing of skills across grades and levels, allocation and reallocation of time throughout the school day and school year, and other issues which have implications for organizational structure and arrangements in schools.

If the conclusions outlined above make it appear that initiation of thinking-skills projects is an imposing challenge not to be undertaken lightly, we have succeeded in communicating our most important overall conclusion. Making sure that such projects are manageable for teachers and that fundamental realities and characteristics of elementary and secondary schools are addressed and modified as part of a thinking-skills project is indeed an enormous burden. Similarly, the need to deal with basic problems in leadership, organizational culture, and related matters as part of a thinking-skills project also means that one should think many more times than twice before deciding to launch an effort to improve instruction aimed at improving thinking and other higher-order skills.

You can see why my introductory comments referred to the task of improving the thinking skills of at-risk students as "overwhelming."

Sixth, *some research is beginning to support the conclusion that various approaches and projects for improving thinking skills have improved the performance of at-risk students*. Several of these approaches and projects are cited below.

1. The *Instrumental Enrichment* approach developed by Feuerstein and his colleagues (Feuerstein et al. 1985) is particularly attractive theoretically because it is specifically intended to provide mediated instruction to improve the cognitive functioning of previously low-achieving students across a wide range of ages. Scholars who have examined data on implementation and outcomes of *Instrumental Enrichment* generally have concluded that early results tend to be positive and encouraging (Brainin 1985; Sternberg 1986; Sternberg and Bhana 1986).

2. *Metacognitive* approaches developed by Brown, Palincsar, and their colleagues (Brown 1985) have produced impressive performance gains by previously low-achieving students. These results are particularly encouraging because the techniques they employed specifically recognize the importance of developing more active learning behaviors and skills among low-achieving students.

123

3. Techniques that Herber (1985) and others have developed to improve *comprehension of material in content areas* also have produced some encouraging data regarding gains among elementary and secondary students in general and among at-risk students in particular. These techniques are particularly promising because they can be used by any teacher in any subject area. In addition, many techniques (e.g., advance organizers, webbing, and concept mapping) are available, from which teachers can select and adapt as appropriate for their particular classrooms (Harris and Cooper 1985).

4. The *Chicago Mastery Learning Reading Program* (CMLRP) (Campione and Armbruster 1985; Jones, Amiran, and Katims 1985) has been an important component in several successful efforts to help low-achieving students master and utilize specific learning strategies and improve their reading comprehension. Reports by Jones and Spady (1985), Levine and Stark (1982), Robb (1985), Thompson (1985), and Williams (1987) indicate that disadvantaged students can achieve large gains in reading when the CMLRP is implemented well as part of a larger effort to reform instruction in elementary or intermediate schools.

5. The *Productive Thinking Program* (PTP), developed by Covington (1985) and his colleagues, has reported encouraging results in teaching problem-solving skills to low achievers (Polson and Jeffries 1985). The PTP appears to be particularly attractive because it explicitly attempts to overcome students' fear of failure.

6. The Higher Order Thinking Skills (HOTS) program, developed by Pogrow (1988) and his colleagues, has produced promising results among low-achieving students in grades four through six. Designed to increase students' conceptual ability through computerized instruction coordinated with the regular classroom, the HOTS program has helped students gain in both reading and mathematics performance.

However, I must also stress that our knowledge base for teaching thinking to at-risk students remains very limited, as is research on teaching higher-order mental processes in general. Developers and researchers are still addressing fundamental questions involving the types of skills that should be emphasized for differing students, effective techniques to sequence and teach these skills, transfer to new situations, assessment of results, and other issues (Chipman, Segal, and Glaser 1985; Segal, Chipman, and Glaser 1985).

Regarding the approaches cited above and others for teaching thinking to low-achieving students, data on implementation and results generally are still fragmentary, assessment instruments used in evalua-

124

tion frequently have been rudimentary or questionable, and little is known concerning long-term effects, sustained implementation, and coordination between cognitive and affective components and goals. (OERI, where are you?) In particular, we need much more research to identify prerequisites for successful implementation. Experimental methods can help us determine whether one approach or another has meaningful effects in comparison with a control group, but they generally do not tell us much about how to implement thinking-skills projects successfully over a lengthy period of time on a widespread basis in typical schools and classrooms.

My seventh generalization also is encouraging: *approaches for improving the thinking skills of at-risk students can be combined to constitute a comprehensive effort to improve their education.* Among the approaches cited above, for example, there does not seem to be any inherent obstacle to productive combinations. The *Instrumental Enrichment* program can be implemented, if one wishes, during a period of time allocated for this purpose at various grades. Metacognitive and other comprehension-development approaches, such as those used by Herber and his colleagues, can be used to deliver regular instruction in content subjects in any grade. The *Chicago Mastery Learning Reading Program* can be used in place of some existing reading/language arts instruction in grades K through eight. And the *Productive Thinking Program* can be allocated a defined block of time in grade five or six. By utilizing these approaches across a common curriculum, we could address a range of thinking-skills objectives including basic cognitive functioning, self-regulation in thinking, acquisition of prior knowledge and schema, mastery of learning strategies, and problem solving.

Personally, I have observed inner-city intermediate schools in which *Chicago Mastery Learning Reading* was an important part of the daily reading period, and a variety of metacognitive and comprehension-development techniques was being used by most teachers in English, history, science, and other subjects. I believe use of these techniques played an important part in helping to generate the large improvements in reading comprehension that were registered at some of these schools.

Of course, I am not advocating that educators seize on and implement every approach available for improving thinking among at-risk students. We must be careful to avoid teacher or school overload and other obstacles to implementation cited above. Differing approaches should be selected and coordinated to address a compatible set of objectives; selection and implementation should, as always, be based on assessment of needs, review of applicable research, and ongoing collection of formative and summative evaluation data. In addition, in working with low achievers, it is particularly important to plan and deliver instruction aimed at coordinating and reinforcing the development of higher-order mental processes across subject areas. Nevertheless, it is encouraging to realize that we have an "arsenal" of promising and potentially compatible approaches for improving the thinking of low achievers. Pearson (1985) has referred to the recent development of some of these approaches as a virtual "revolution" in our pedagogical capabilities.

SPECULATIONS

I have labeled the topics considered in this section speculative because relevant generalizations and conclusions are not as well established as are those in the preceding section. In some cases, we are only beginning to formulate useful questions regarding the teaching of higher-order skills to low-achieving students. The topics I will briefly discuss in this section are these: the relationship between basic skills and thinking skills, bilingual education, learning styles, school structure, and instructional planning time/instructional support personnel.

Basic Skills

In using the term *basic skills*, I refer to relatively mechanical and fact-oriented skills such as decoding, spelling, and grammar in reading; computation in mathematics; chronology and location facts in history and geography; and terminology in science. Fact-oriented mastery appears to be the most frequently used working definition of basic skills, though some authors (e.g., Sizemore 1985) extend the term to include thinking and other higher-order skills.

One should not reject out of hand the importance of basic skills instruction in working to improve the performance of low achievers. As pointed out by Good (1987), Rosenshine and Stevens (1986), and others, students must become fluent in some basic skills in order to acquire the knowledge foundation they need for higher-order processing and application of information. In addition, mastery of basic skills can help low achievers develop an improved self-concept as learners and enhance their motivation to succeed in school. On the other hand, some studies (e.g., Soled 1987) indicate that students are likely to learn and remember as much or more factual content when instruction focuses on higher-order mental processes as when it emphasizes low-level mechanical learning.

In addition, it appears that overemphasis on basic skills is an unproductive substitute for instruction to develop low achievers' higher-order skills in many schools and classrooms. The Commission on Reading (Anderson et al. 1985) concluded that American students spend too much time completing workbooks and worksheets that concentrate on basic skills; the Commission recommended that these activities "be

126

pared to the minimum" (p. 119) that actually provides worthwhile practice in reading. As the Commission and others (e.g., Wick and Turnbaugh 1983; Davy and Macready 1986) have pointed out, competence in understanding text does not consist of a large number of discrete subskills that one can master and combine mechanically through extensive practice in workbooks. This conclusion agrees with my own observations, and with those of nearly all the knowledgeable observers with whom I have discussed this topic in recent years. The most direct victims of overemphasis on basic skills frequently are low achievers, whose time is often diverted to still more worksheets while high achievers proceed to more meaningful and integrated learning experiences (Shavelson 1983).

The reasons for overemphasizing basic skills are not at all mysterious. In addition to the fact that ill-advised accountability schemes drive instruction toward the most easily measured skills, many teachers prefer emphasizing basic skills that are relatively easy to teach and test. Many students not only prefer low-level basic skills instruction, but also openly resist anything different (Doyle 1983). And classroom order is easier to maintain when students are preoccupied with, or encouraged to give the appearance of being preoccupied with, worksheets. Overcoming unproductive overemphasis on basic skills will require massive attention, resources, and action to deal with this set of interrelated phenomena in the schools.

I characterize this topic as speculative primarily because no one, as far as I know, has provided clear and specific information and guidelines to determine how much basic skills instruction students must receive to develop the fluency they need for subsequent higher-order processing. At this point in time, we do not even seem to know what kinds of basic skills gains translate into later improvements in thinking and other higher-order skills, or under what conditions that is likely to occur. My own opinion is that helping low achievers master a carefully selected and numerically limited set of criterion-referenced skills frequently does translate into later gains in standardized tests of reading comprehension, mathematics concepts, and problem solving, provided that appropriate instruction is provided subsequently. My major bases for this conclusion are observations and data I collected in 1980–1981 at unusually effective inner-city elementary schools in Los Angeles. However, we must consider the larger questions raised by this discussion as fundamentally wide open for researchers in the future.

Bilingual Education

Don't get alarmed: I do not intend to review the enormous literature on bilingual education. Instead, I will briefly call attention to several intriguing indications that a central problem in teaching non-English-proficient (NEP) and limited-English-proficient (LEP) students may be an overemphasis on mastery of basic skills and a concomitant neglect of comprehension, thinking, and other higher-order processes. Stated differently, typical implementations of bilingual approaches providing instruction in the students' native language and of immersion-oriented approaches providing instruction entirely or largely in English may be emphasizing low-level mechanical skills.

Some evidence in support of this conclusion has been provided by Cazden (1985), who analyzed data collected in the Significant Bilingual Instructional Features (SBIF) study and concluded (1) that Spanish-to-English transitional programs frequently place too much emphasis on decoding, as compared with comprehension, and (2) that instruction in both languages tends to repeat the same low-level mechanical skills.

Regarding instruction in immersion-oriented approaches, it certainly is not difficult to believe that much of the instruction provided in English for NEP and LEP students may be neglecting higher-order skills. After all, how different would this be from instruction typically provided for low achievers in general? Lack of attention to higher-order skills was determined to be a pervasive problem in one study of an English-language reading class for Spanish-speaking third graders who had attained some proficiency in English (Moll, Estrada, Diaz, and Lopes, reported by Simmons 1985). Simmons summarizes some of the conclusions from this study as follows:

> The second-language environments were organized to focus primarily on lower level "mechanical" tasks such as decoding skills, phonics, and simple language development activities. Practically absent from the middle and high groups in English were the types of directing activities or mediating strategies that characterized these groups in the more advanced first-language classroom. (p. 530)

Additional support for this interpretation has been provided in a recent analysis of bilingual education by Hakuta and Gould (1987). After reviewing research on instructional methods for NEP/LEP students, Hakuta and Gould concluded that children learning a second language need several years to acquire fluency sufficient to function at a "decontextualized" level in the language. If so, students in transit from native-language classes to classes in English may not be adequately prepared to participate in instruction focused on higher mental processing, regardless of whether or not previous instruction in the native language overemphasized mechanical skills.

Learning Styles

As in the case of bilingual education, I will not attempt to provide a comprehensive review of research; instead, I will identify only a few issues concerning the role of learning styles in teaching thinking to low achievers. Research supports the conclusion that students differ in modal learning style (Presseisen 1986), and there is some support for the conclusion that instruction adapted to a student's learning style can improve his or her learning (Carbo, Dunn, and Dunn 1986). However, instruction based on learning-style differences generally has not raised achievement levels (Doyle and Rutherford 1984), and it presently is difficult to advocate any particular approach to improving higher-order skills through instruction adapted to learning styles. My reasons for reaching this judgment follow:

- Few studies that assess the impact of learning-styles instruction have distinguished between acquisition of mechanical and higher-order skills, or have paid particular attention to higher-order skills. Similarly, studies of modal transformations from one expressive mode to another which have been conducted with low-achieving students have not been adequate.

- Some learning-styles approaches postulate that initial instruction for many students, including many low achievers, should concentrate on concrete, small-step learning tasks and experiences. While it probably is true that many low achievers learn best initially from concrete, small-step instruction, approaches that explicitly or implicitly utilize this theory generally do not provide for systematic movement to more abstract, higher-level learning. This deficiency raises the possibility that some learning-styles approaches may be counterproductive in reinforcing rather than diminishing tendencies toward overemphasis on mechanical learning.

- Some learning-styles approaches are quite elaborate and consequently have a high PFMQ (Potential for Mischief Quotient) when implemented in the typical school or classroom (Doyle and Rutherford 1984). Among these are approaches that urge teachers to consider or respond to forty or fifty or a hundred or more differing aspects of learning preferences among students. Such approaches are sometimes a virtual recipe for disaster when placed in the hands of the many administrators and supervisors who seem to ignore the difficulties teachers face in delivering differentiated instruction effectively in the classroom.

I hope that this brief discussion—based impressionistically on observation in schools and on frequent exposure to articles and studies dealing with learning styles, but not on a complete review and assessment of available research—has not been overly unfair to learning-style advocates. I certainly would welcome more good research and reviews of research on the role of learning styles in improving thinking skills among low achievers.

129

In addition, I must report that in my own experience some schools have made good use of learning-styles theory to improve the effectiveness of instruction for low-achieving students. For example, elementary and middle schools in Johnson City, New York, have implemented a mastery learning approach that requires teachers to present corrective instruction in a different mode than the initial lesson (Mamary and Rowe 1985). This simple policy, which is highly manageable by the teacher, appears to have played a part in bringing about very large gains in student achievement. In general, educators who have been using learning-styles research successfully in Johnson City and other locations seem to have avoided elaborate efforts to adapt instruction comprehensively to each student's varied learning preferences.

School Structure

As indicated above, my review of research on implications of the change process for projects to improve students' thinking concluded that we will have to stress the revision of organizational arrangements and structures in elementary and secondary schools. Modification of organizational structures and arrangements is particularly critical in improving the performance of low-achieving students in inner-city secondary schools, which I define as schools enrolling a significant proportion of students from economically disadvantaged families. It is hard to see how we can substantially improve the thinking skills of low achievers in inner-city intermediate or senior high schools as long as we deliver instruction through traditional structures. Changing those structures and improving them as climates for learning seem to comprise a necessary first step (Levine and Eubanks 1988).

An example of the kinds of organizational changes that are needed is the School-Within-a-School (SWAS) program established for low-achieving ninth-graders in the Kansas City (Missouri) senior high schools. Designed for students with reading scores roughly between the fourth-grade and eighth-grade levels,* the SWAS program usually assigns eighty to one hundred students to receive academic instruction from four or five teachers, including teachers of English, mathematics, reading, social studies, and, in some cases, science. A teacher coordinator who serves at least half-time has also been appointed. Working within this structure, the teachers are provided with training and other forms of assistance to implement the following program goals and components:

- Content area materials utilized are below students' frustration level

---

*Ninth-graders reading below the fourth-grade level require a different, even stronger intervention.

for independent work and slightly above their instructional level for classroom instruction.

- Instructional methods emphasize comprehension-development techniques, such as those described by Herber (1985), and active learning approaches, such as Student Team Learning.
- Personal attention is provided for students by a limited number of carefully selected teachers, and close contact is maintained, if possible, with parents.
- Teachers have common planning periods and are given training intended to improve the coordination of instruction, particularly in order to reinforce curriculum and instruction across classes.

The School-Within-a-School structure has given teachers some important advantages as they work to improve the comprehension of participating students. These advantages include the following:

- The teachers selected are particularly willing and skilled in working with low achievers.
- The program facilitates the provision of a variety of motivating and personal development activities for students.
- Such a group of dedicated teachers can frequently survive the annual crises that predictably disrupt urban high schools.
- Manageable arrangements allow emphasis on development of comprehension, thinking, and other higher-order skills.

When implemented properly, the Kansas City SWAS program and other similar approaches can be very effective. Among ninth-grade units in Kansas City, for example, impressive gains have been registered in student attendance, performance on state-mandated basic skills tests, and, in some cases, achievement in reading comprehension.

Although I have no hesitancy in concluding that fundamental changes are needed in the organizational structure of inner-city secondary schools, the situation in schools with only a small proportion of low achievers is not as clear. It is possible that we can bring about substantial improvements in teaching thinking and other higher-order skills to at-risk students at these schools, even within largely traditional arrangements. In fact, providing adequate and appropriate additional assistance for low achievers through tutoring and other means may be more feasible in economically mixed intermediate and senior high schools than in inner-city schools in which the magnitude of this task virtually overwhelms the traditional structure. On the other hand, there also is reason to believe that fundamental changes in structure can help promote achievement gains for all groups of students at any secondary school, regardless of its socioeconomic composition and current achievement level (Levine and Sherk 1983; Sizer 1984).

Instructional Planning Time / Instructional Support Personnel

The instructional approaches discussed above can result in large achievement gains among previously low achievers, particularly with regard to their performance on higher-order skills such as comprehension in reading and other subjects and problem solving in mathematics. Unfortunately, the "downside" of this development is that teachers need considerable technical assistance and other forms of help if they are to use these improved instructional approaches effectively. As summarized by MacGinitie and MacGinitie (1986), the situation today is basically that "There is essentially nothing in instructional materials or in teacher training [of the past] that helps the teacher learn what to do when the child does not understand" (p. 258).

Bolstering teachers' capacity to deliver effective instruction to improve thinking and other higher-order skills of low achievers will require not only a great deal of staff development time but also substantial instructional planning time on a regular basis and assistance from support personnel who work with teachers in their own classrooms. Regarding instructional planning time, a good rule of thumb is one I advanced elsewhere in an essay on successful implementation of mastery learning (Levine 1985): observe and talk with teachers who are implementing important changes in curriculum and instruction, prepare a liberal estimate of the amount of planning time you require, and then double your estimate. Regarding instructional support personnel, no research to date explicitly addresses the amount of resources required. I can only guess that adequate technical assistance aimed at improving thinking skills among low achievers initially will require one full-time equivalent specialist for every fifteen to twenty-five teachers, depending on the nature of the project, the experience of the teachers, and other considerations.

WORRIES

Rather than proceeding for endless pages to discuss all the plausible pitfalls likely to be encountered in projects to improve thinking and other higher-order skills among low achievers, I will limit myself to listing, with little explanation, a few of the most prominent and worrisome tendencies—those for which we should be particularly vigilant.

First, some thinking-skills approaches lend themselves to mechanical misimplementation and maladministration because they identify and categorize a large number of skills and subskills thought to comprise critical thinking, problem solving, metacognitive self-regulation, or other aspects of thinking. Placing such lists at the disposal of some state legislators, school board members, or district administrators unfortunately is likely to result in the same kind of by-the-numbers substitute for effective teaching that we recently have seen with respect to mastery learning and direct instruction approaches in many locations.

Related to this concern, I also worry about the dilemmas posed by manageability considerations on the one hand and tendencies to depend too much on prepackaged materials on the other. Packaged materials to teach thinking can help make a project manageable for teachers, but the introduction of materials seems to lead many administrators to confuse beginnings with complete solutions.

Third, there is a danger that educators will fixate on one approach or another and insist on blind adherence to it at a time when we are only beginning to understand how various approaches should be organized, and sometimes combined, for effective implementation in the classroom. McNamara (1987) of the Philadelphia public schools has described and discussed how this tendency has hampered the development of Follow Through approaches, and has concluded that "we should abandon trying to resolve educational problems by insisting on faithful adherence to far-reaching philosophical or over-arching theoretical positions and spend more time trying to work middle range theories" (p. 16). Similar recommendations are in order concerning the development of thinking-skills projects for at-risk students, particularly because we are seldom able in educational research to determine with much confidence why a given approach has or has not worked; the extent to which it succeeded because of extraneous, unrecognized considerations, or failed because of misimplementation; or the precise prerequisites to successful implementation.

Fourth, the depth of our advocacy for programs to improve higher-order learning among low achievers may lead us to neglect the profound obstacles we will encounter in moving to fundamentally improve instruction in the classroom. Sternberg (1986) recently emphasized this concern in summarizing his own experience with respect to a thinking-skills project at inner-city schools:

...a successful marriage between cognitive theory and instructional practice may be possible [only if] certain potential stumbling blocks are taken into account. It is better to take these things into account and to attempt to deal with them before the program is implemented than to wait until a later postmortem that seeks to discover just what went wrong in the implementation of a program. (p. 382)

Finally, I am very worried that preoccupation with the technical issues involved in teaching thinking to at-risk students will reinforce tendencies to neglect important issues involving the larger educational opportunities available to them. Earlier in this chapter, I cited the conclusions of a few among the many scholars who have emphasized the importance of motivation in working to develop higher-order skills. For many at-risk students, sustained improvements in motivation ultimately will be dependent on the success of our efforts to "deghettoize" and deconcentrate poverty in big city schools.

DISCUSSION QUESTIONS

1. If we are to successfully teach thinking to at-risk students, what knowledge about the change process in educational institutions do we need to follow at the same time?

2. How does the goal of teaching higher-level thinking to at-risk students relate to arguments about bilingual education? What general research findings are available in this area?

3. Why does the controversy over learning style approaches prevent educators from getting a clear picture of this concept and its relevance to teaching higher-order thinking skills to at-risk students?

4. What are the negative possibilities of teaching higher-level thinking to at-risk students, and how can they be countered?

REFERENCES

Anderson, R. C.; Hiebert, E. H.; Scott, J. A.; and Wilkinson, I. A. G. 1985. *Becoming a nation of readers: The report of the Commission on Reading.* Washington, D.C.: National Institute of Education.

Baron, J. 1985. What kinds of intelligence components are fundamental? In *Thinking and learning skills.* Vol. 2, *Research and open questions*, ed. S. F. Chipman, J. W. Segal, and R. Glaser. Hillsdale, N.J.: Lawrence Erlbaum Associates.

Brainin, S. S. 1985. Mediated learning: Pedagogic issues in the improvement of cognitive functioning. In *Review of research in education.* Vol. 12, ed. E. W. Gordon, 121-55. Washington, D.C.: American Educational Research Association.

Brown, A. L. 1985. Mental orthopedics, the training of cognitive skills: An interview with Alfred Binet. In *Thinking and learning skills.* Vol. 2, *Research and open questions*, ed. S. F. Chipman, J. W. Segal, and R. Glaser. Hillsdale, N.J.: Lawrence Erlbaum Associates.

Bruner, J. 1985. On teaching thinking: An afterthought. In *Thinking and learning skills.* Vol. 2, *Research and open questions*, ed. S. F. Chipman, J. W. Segal, and R. Glaser. Hillsdale, N.J.: Lawrence Erlbaum Associates.

Campione, J. C., and Armbruster, B. B. 1985. Acquiring information from texts: An analysis of four approaches. In *Thinking and learning skills.* Vol. 1, *Relating instruction to research*, ed. J. W. Segal, S. F. Chipman, and R. Glaser. Hillsdale, N.J.: Lawrence Erlbaum Associates.

Carbo, M.; Dunn, R.; and Dunn, K. 1986. *Teaching students to read through individual learning styles.* Englewood Cliffs, N.J.: Prentice-Hall.

Case, R. 1985. A developmentally based approach to the problem of instructional design. In *Thinking and learning skills*. Vol. 2, *Research and open questions,* ed. S F. Chipman, J. W. Segal, and R. Glaser. Hillsdale, N.J.: Lawrence Erlbaum Associates.

Cazden, C. B. 1985. Effective instructional practices in bilingual education. Paper presented at the annual meeting of the American Educational Research Association, Chicago.

Chipman, S. F.; Segal, J. W.; and Glaser, R., eds. 1985. *Thinking and learning skills.* Vol. 2, *Research and open questions.* Hillsdale, N.J.: Lawrence Erlbaum Associates.

Covington, M. V. 1985. Strategic thinking and the fear of failure. In *Thinking and learning skills*. Vol. 1, *Relating instruction to research*, ed. J. W. Segal, S. F. Chipman, and R. Glaser. Hillsdale, N.J.: Lawrence Erlbaum Associates.

Davy, B., and Macready, G. B. 1986. Specification and validation of reading comprehension components for good and poor readers. Paper presented at the annual meeting of the American Educational Research Association, San Francisco.

Doyle, W. 1983. Academic work. *Review of Educational Research* 53(2): 159–99.

Doyle, W., and Rutherford, B. 1984. Classroom research on matching learning and teaching styles. *Theory into Practice* 23(1): 21–25.

Feuerstein, R.; Jensen, M. R.; Hoffman, M. B.; and Rand, Y. 1985. Instrumental enrichment, an intervention program for structural cognitive modifiability: Theory and practice. In *Thinking and learning skills*. Vol. 1, *Relating instruction to research*, ed. J. W. Segal, S. F. Chipman, and R. Glaser, 43–82. Hillsdale, N.J.: Lawrence Erlbaum Associates.

Good, T. L. 1987. Two decades of research on teacher expectations: Findings and future directions. *Journal of Teacher Education* 38(4): 32–47.

Goodlad, J. I. 1984. *A place called school.* New York: McGraw-Hill.

Hakuta, K., and Gould, L. J. 1987. Synthesis of research on bilingual education. *Educational Leadership* 44(6): 38–45.

Harris, T. L., and Cooper, E. J., eds. 1985. *Reading, thinking, and concept development: Strategies for the classroom.* New York: College Entrance Examination Board.

Herber, H. L. 1985. Developing reading and thinking skills in content areas. In *Thinking and learning skills*. Vol. 1, *Relating instruction to research*, ed. J. W. Segal, S. F. Chipman, and R. Glaser. Hillsdale, N.J.: Lawrence Erlbaum Associates.

Jones, B. F. 1986. Quality and equality through cognitive instruction. *Educational Leadership* 43(7): 5–11.

Jones, B F.; Amiran, M.; and Katims, M. 1985. Teaching cognitive strategies and text structures. In *Thinking and learning skills*. Vol. 1, *Relating instruction to research*, ed. J. W. Segal, S. F. Chipman, and R. Glaser. Hillsdale, N.J.: Lawrence Erlbaum Associates.

Jones, B. F., and Spady, W. G. 1985. Enhanced mastery learning as a solution to the two sigma problem. In *Improving student achievement through mastery learning programs*, ed. D. U. Levine. San Francisco: Jossey-Bass.

Levine, D. U., ed. 1985. *Improving student achievement through mastery learning programs.* San Francisco: Jossey-Bass.

Levine, D. U., and Cooper, E. J. In press. The change process and its implications in teaching thinking. In *Dimensions of thinking and cognitive instruction,* ed. B. F. Jones and L. Idol. Hillsdale, N.J.: Lawrence Erlbaum Associates.

Levine, D. U.; and Eubanks, E. E. 1988. Organizational arrangements at effective secondary schools. In *Organizing for learning*, ed. J. J. Lane and H. W. Walberg. Reston, Va.: National Association of Secondary School Principals.

Levine, D. U., and Havighurst, R. J. 1988. *Society and education*. 7th ed. Newton, Mass.: Allyn & Bacon.

Levine, D. U., and Sherk, J. K. 1983. Organizational arrangements to increase productive time for reading in high schools. Paper prepared for the International Reading Association.

Levine, D. U., and Stark, J. 1982. Instructional and organizational arrangements that improve achievement at inner city schools. *Educational Leadership* 40(3): 41–46.

MacGinitie, W. H., and MacGinitie, R. K. 1986. Teaching students not to read. In *Literacy, society, and schooling*, ed. S. deCastell, A. Luke, and K. Egan. Cambridge, England: Cambridge University Press.

McNamara, T. 1987. A large school district's perspective on the structure controversy. Paper presented at the annual meeting of the American Educational Research Association, Washington, D.C.

Mamary, A., and Rowe, L. A. 1985. Flexible and heterogeneous instructional arrangements to facilitate mastery learning. In *Improving student achievement through mastery learning programs*, ed. D. U. Levine. San Francisco: Jossey-Bass.

Marzano, R. J.; Brandt, R.; Hughes, C.; Jones, B. F.; Presseisen, B. Z.; Rankin, S.; and Suhor, C. 1988. *Dimensions of thinking: A framework for curriculum and instruction*. Alexandria, Va.: Association for Supervision and Curriculum Development.

Meichenbaum, D. 1985. Teaching thinking: A cognitive-behavioral model. In *Thinking and learning skills*. Vol. 2, *Research and open questions*, ed. S. F. Chipman, J. W. Segal, and R. Glaser. Hillsdale, N.J.: Lawrence Erlbaum Associates.

Nickerson, R. S.; Perkins, D. N.; and Smith, E. E. 1985. The *teaching of thinking*. Hillsdale, N.J.: Lawrence Erlbaum Associates.

Pearson, D. P. 1985. The comprehension revolution: A twenty-year history of process and practice related to reaching comprehension. Report no. 57. Urbana: University of Illinois at Urbana-Champaign, Center for the Study of Reading.

Pogrow, S. 1988. Teaching thinking to at-risk elementary students. *Educational Leadership* 45(7): 79–85.

Polson, P. G., and Jeffries, R. 1985. Instruction in general problem-solving skills: An analysis of four approaches. In *Thinking and learning skills*. Vol. 1, *Relating instruction to research*, ed. J. W. Segal, S. F. Chipman, and R. Glaser. Hillsdale, N.J.: Lawrence Erlbaum Associates.

Porter, A. C.; Floden, R. E.; Freeman, D. J.; Schmidt, W. H.; and Schwille, J. R. 1986. *Content determinants*. Research Series no. 179. East Lansing: Michigan State University, Institute for Research on Teaching.

Presseisen, B. Z. 1986. *Thinking skills: Research and practice*. Washington, D.C.: National Education Association.

Putnam, J.; Roehler, L. R.; and Duffy, G. R. 1987. *The staff development model of the teacher explanation project*. Occasional Paper no. 108. East Lansing: Michigan State University, Institute for Research on Teaching.

Robb, D. W. 1985. Strategies for implementing successful mastery learning programs: Case studies. In *Improving student achievement through mastery learning programs*, ed. D. U. Levine. San Francisco: Jossey-Bass.

Rosenshine, B., and Stevens, R. 1986. Teaching functions. In *Handbook of research on teaching*, ed. M. C. Wittrock. 3d ed. New York: Macmillan.

Scardamalia, M., and Bereiter, C. 1985. Fostering the development of self-regulation in children's knowledge processing. In *Thinking and learning skills*. Vol. 2, *Research and open questions*, ed. S. F. Chipman, J. W. Segal, and R. Glaser. Hillsdale, N.J.: Lawrence Erlbaum Associates.

Sedlak, M. W.; Wheeler, C. W.; Pullin, D. C.; and Cusick, P. A. 1986. *Selling students short*. New York: Teachers College Press.

Segal, J. W.; Chipman, S. F.; and Glaser, R., eds. 1985. *Thinking and learning skills*. Vol. 1, *Relating instruction to research*. Hillsdale, N.J.: Lawrence Erlbaum Associates.

Shavelson, R. J. 1985. Schemata and teaching routines. Paper presented at the annual meeting of the American Educational Research Association, Chicago.

Simmons, W. 1985. Social class and ethnic differences in cognition: A cultural practice perspective. In *Thinking and learning skills*. Vol. 2, *Research and open questions*, ed. S. F. Chipman, J. W. Segal, and R. Glaser. Hillsdale, N.J.: Lawrence Erlbaum Associates.

Sizemore, B. A. 1985. Pitfalls and promises of effective schools research. *Journal of Negro Education* 54:269–88.

Sizer, T. R. 1984. *Horace's compromise: The dilemma of the American high school*. Boston: Houghton Mifflin.

Soled, S. W. 1987. Teaching processes to improve both higher as well as lower mental process achievement. Paper presented at the annual meeting of the American Educational Research Association, Washington, D.C.

Sternberg, R. J. 1986. Cognition and instruction: Why the marriage sometimes ends in divorce. In *Cognition and instruction*, ed. R. F. Dillon and R. J. Sternberg, 375–82. Orlando, Fla.: Academic Press.

Sternberg, R. J., and Bhana, K. 1986. Synthesis of research on the effectiveness of intellectual skills programs: Snake-oil remedies or miracle cures? *Educational Leadership* 44(2): 61–67.

Thompson, W. E. 1985. A practitioner's perspective on the Chicago Mastery Learning Program with learning strategies. In *Thinking and learning skills*. Vol. 1, *Relating instruction to research*, ed. J. W. Segal, S. F. Chipman, and R. Glaser. Hillsdale, N.J.: Lawrence Erlbaum Associates.

Weinstein, C. E., and Mayer, R. E. 1986. The teaching of learning strategies. In *Handbook of research on teaching*. 3d ed., ed. M. C. Wittrock, 315–27. New York: Macmillan.

Wick, J. K., and Turnbaugh, R. C. 1983. *A successful program to improve student performance*. Evanston, Ill.: Northwestern University, Division of Field Studies.

Williams, B. 1987. Implementing thinking skills instruction in an urban district: An effort to close the gap. *Educational Leadership* 44(6): 50–53.

8. STRATEGIES TO HELP TEACHERS EMPOWER AT-RISK STUDENTS

by Jill A. Mirman, Robert J. Swartz, and John Barell

At-risk students provide a lens through which we see an educational system that is not working across the board. We can put this observation into context by taking an objective, historical pose that recognizes this is not just the way things are and always have to be. We are in a new phase of change and development during which we are setting lofty goals for ourselves—goals we have yet to reach. As we revamp America's educational system, no area is more significant for teaching thinking than the preparation of teachers.

IMPROVEMENT FOR ALL

America's goal is to provide a quality education for *all* children, regardless of the disadvantage they bring with them to the classroom door—social, economic, academic, linguistic, behavioral, cognitive, and so on. "[Q]uality education is the central civil rights challenge facing us today. To realize the goal of equal opportunity generally, we must provide our students with equal intellectual opportunity in school" (Bennett 1988).

In this chapter, we will discuss processes for improving education, beginning with specific classroom strategies that will give at-risk students more control over their thinking and their lives. Thereafter, we will show how these same strategies can help teachers and administrators reorganize the school for more collaborative problem solving. However, we realize that a linear approach such as this inaccurately reflects the complex, interactive processes of change.

A high school teacher known to one of the authors was recently challenging a group of disaffected, alienated, underachieving students to engage in more complex thinking processes. Suddenly, one student raised his hand to ask the teacher, "Why are you bothering with all of this?" The teacher, a little stunned, replied, "What do you mean?" The student replied, "Don't you know we are the kids who aren't supposed to learn?"

Throughout this chapter we propose a partial remedy for the needs of these at-risk youths: a quality education undergirded by the teaching of thinking. We believe that by teaching at-risk children to think carefully and independently through decisions and problems, we will help them see that they have choices, that they have some control over their lives. If we teach disadvantaged students in an atmosphere of high expectations and active engagement with and manipulation of knowledge, we will contribute to moving them from the realm of the victim to that of the advantaged. "[In American society] the advantaged individual is the one who can make rational decisions that minimize both risk and randomness. The advantaged person can maintain control amid uncertainty" (Pellicano 1987, p. 48).

We will outline instructional, curricular, and organizational strategies that focus on empowering at-risk students to take more control of their educational and personal lives. These strategies, broadly conceived as an infusion approach to emphasizing thinking in the classroom, will include such specific challenges as sharing control of decision making, setting goals, collaborating in problem solving, improving metacognitive awareness, and finding ways of relating life experiences beyond the classroom to those within the classroom.

Who Is At Risk?

At risk and *thinking* have become rubber terms in our current usage. That is, people use them liberally and yet mean very different things. To make these terms meaningful for the preparation of teachers, we must define the group of children whom we are letting down in our educational system and what is actually meant by the teaching of thinking.

In Chapter 7, Levine, citing the important work of Brainin, suggests that *Instrumental Enrichment* (Feuerstein 1980) is a program that provides a paradigm for teaching thinking to at-risk students. This program, however, is designed primarily for cognitively impaired students, and its instructional strategies are shaped with this audience in mind. We interpret the situation a little differently. Using the discussions of other authors as a foundation, we state clearly that at-risk students are not the same population as special needs and/or otherwise cognitively impaired students; rather, they are youngsters who have more problems with esteem and motivation. We want to emphasize that the problems faced by at-risk students do not stem from cognitive disorders, even though the students we are concerned about typically do not engage the thinking capacities they have with the content we try to teach them in school. Later in this chapter we lay out a curricular and reorganizational approach to teaching thinking that we believe is more effective in its holistic and demanding nature because at-risk students may be characterized differently than the paradigms found in programs such as *Instrumental Enrichment*.

Levin (1987) and other researchers have asserted that school may not be working for as much as 70 percent of our students. This presents a picture of a general problem of schooling. The most commonly discussed aspect of this problem can been seen in urban areas where large numbers of children are not completing high school, where dropping out is the standard operating procedure. A population shift in many urban school districts has caused minorities to become the majority. This demographic phenomenon requires a reshaping of schools to include courses, structures, and supports that accommodate the very special needs of urban minority youngsters. Among the changes called for are a climate of valuing differences, strategies to involve parents who may not speak English as a first language or who do not relate to the dominant school culture, an increase in minority teachers and in language courses of all kinds, and the creation of alternative educational environments (alternative schools, minischools, and schools-within-schools). The latter approach has been tried and proved viable in many large urban areas, such as New York City.

It is not just youngsters in urban areas who are at risk. The needs of families and children in rural areas have changed dramatically, too, and these changes are having a profound effect on American schooling. In one rural area there is a third-grade teacher who has 33 children in his class. As if this ratio alone weren't overwhelming, 15 of his students have parents who are going through or who have in the last year gone through a divorce. That is nearly 50 percent. This teacher says that at a time when his students need that magical combination of nurturing and academic attention—to form the bridge between early elementary grades and middle elementary maturity—he is simply trying to make sure that, at the end of the day, he releases the right child to the right parent and does not get accused of fouling up a custody agreement. This veteran teacher is energetic and enthusiastic; he has sought out information on teaching thinking. But, in order for him to be the effective teacher he can be, he needs a much different support system from his school and his community than he gets now.

The at-risk student population does not merely include the constituency of dropouts in our nation's schools. Students whom we think of as underachievers comprise an often overlooked group of at-risk youngsters. These students only fail parts of school, may be absent frequently, or do not really engage in their school's academic or extracurricular offerings. They know enough about the school "game" to conform quietly—and, thus, they slip unnoticed through the cracks.

Powell and his associates (Powell, Farrar, and Cohen 1985) refer to these underachievers as "the unspecial," and it is clear from their descriptions that the line between them and the students who drop out is quite thin. These unspecial students do not come only from disadvantaged families or from families who do not try to motivate their children. We know of a mid-level manager who works for one of the largest family restaurants and ice cream distributors in New England. Of his three sons, two have followed his and his wife's path of traditional success in school and have gone, or are going, to college. Their middle son, however, has never seemed to enjoy school. His parents know he is of normal intelligence, but he complains that what he learns in school seems to have no relevance for him. He never seems to have an opportunity to explore or write about what interests him, which, in this case, means cars of all sorts and ages. He is not a behavior problem in school and has slipped quietly along to his senior year with an occasional "D" and very few "A"s and "B"s. On his report cards teachers say that he is not working up to his potential, but no one at the school has proposed any solution to this problem. His father is very active in the local school system and, ironically, has been a leader in forming partnerships between the schools and area businesses to help prevent high school students from dropping out. Yet he does not know what to do to motivate his own son and does not understand what the school does for "kids in the middle." At-risk students include those who find little meaning in schooling; when they are also poverty stricken, they are even more endangered.

AN EFFECTIVE APPROACH TO TEACHING THINKING TO AT-RISK STUDENTS

We believe curricular infusion is the most effective approach for teaching thinking to at-risk students. By this we mean integrating the teaching of thinking into standard subject-area instruction. This restructuring of the way traditional content is taught links thinking processes with subject-matter content. Such a link makes sense in our current schooling because the subject areas need thinking to make them more meaningful, and thinking needs content to provide something to think about. Furthermore, as teachers are preparing themselves to teach content, they can become skilled in relating their subjects to particular ways of thinking.

A major aim of the curricular infusion approach is to make the content knowledge taught in school more meaningful and relevant to students. As Wehlage and Rutter (1986) point out, although the pervasive characteristic of at-risk youngsters is failure, their underlying problems are really alienation and boredom. These students feel little connection between school and their own reality. When asked to reflect on the comparison between schooling and life beyond school walls, they make comments such as this: "You think outside of school. . . .here you learn and memorize stuff!" It is not only a cognitive mismatch but also

141

a personal one that highlights the discrepancy between life and schooling. As Eisner (1988) notes, "Whatever [students] are as people gets dropped by the door as they come in and picked up again as they leave."

This discrepancy leads us to conclude that infused instructional strategies such as setting goals, posing and resolving problems collaboratively, and involving students in sharing control of decision making will be (and have been observed to be) effective not only for average students but for at-risk students as well. This approach aims to address such special characteristics of at-risk students as—

- feeling that what is taught in school has little relevance to their lives;
- experiencing detachment from school;
- lacking motivation;
- having low self-esteem; and
- encountering problems in making cognitive connections across subjects and between school learning and real life.

Further, we suggest that the active role students take in thinking deeply about what is being taught and in applying thinking strategies to topics outside school helps them transfer what they have learned to other relevant contexts. Newmann's (1987) recent research supports this point. Teaching metacognition is another key operation of this suggested approach. Teaching students to think about their own thinking helps them reflect on many aspects of their lives and enables them to transfer this skill to a variety of other situations.

When students have opportunities to manipulate information and create ideas in a climate that encourages the generation of knowledge—not just the consumption of knowledge—their motivation increases (Brophy and Good 1984). Thus, the classroom climate that sends a message of high expectations can also increase self-esteem.

At this point we will offer an example of the infused strategies we deem especially appropriate for at-risk students: infusing specific thinking skills, sharing control, setting goals, solving problems collaboratively, increasing metacognitive awareness, and strengthening the links between experiences in and out of school.

An Example of Infusion

This sample of infusion will help illustrate some of these points.

Teaching for Critical Thinking

Teachers who have worked to infuse critical thinking in their own teaching learn that it is neither esoteric, nor technically difficult. It tends to bring out their best abilities, as well as those of their students. Kevin O'Reilly, for example, is a high school American history teacher from the Hamilton-Wenham school system. To teach about the reliability of sources of information in history, he stages a scuffle in the corridors outside his classroom and then asks student witnesses to tell what happened. He compares the accounts his students give to the variety of accounts that were given about the Battle of Lexington in 1775, which started the Revolutionary War. As these students attempt to determine which of the eyewitnesses gave the most accurate account and reflect on why one historical account is better or worse than another, they are armed with critical skills that they draw on again and again in O'Reilly's classroom. These skills relate to the reliability and accuracy of eyewitnesses, of observation, and of sources of information in general—skills of great importance in our lives outside of the classroom. In the immediate context of their study of the Revolutionary War, O'Reilly's students use these skills to make informed critical judgments about the accuracy of various textbook accounts of the Lexington incident that students who are simply directed to read to "get the facts" cannot make. (Swartz 1986, p. 43)

We should note the deliberate attempt in this lesson to assimilate a nonacademic experience (the simulated scuffle in the hall) with a similar phenomenon in history. The teacher draws the connection to give personalized "meaningfulness" to the study of the historical material (Mayer 1975). Furthermore, practicing eyewitness reporting "in person" helps students assess the reports presented about the battle and enhances their motivation to engage with information about it. Finally, the holistic problem approach to examining the battle helps give students a framework within which discrete facts become more meaningful and are easier to retain.

This approach has been used successfully across various subjects and with grades K–12. It requires real change from the ways in which most teachers currently teach. These changes and how teachers need to be supported in making them will be discussed later in this chapter.

SHARING CONTROL OF POWER WITH STUDENTS

One of the most fundamental reasons that students are labeled at risk results from the nature of schooling: most students have very little control over their own educational processes throughout elementary, middle, and high school and college. They have few opportunities to make decisions that will directly affect their fate within the educational environment (Sarason 1971; Fullan 1982).

Finding opportunities for students to share in the control of the environment and/or the curricular options is one strategy that works with all students because everybody wants to have a stake in what they are doing. Some practical ways of providing these opportunities include the following:

1. Involve students in making class rules from the first day of school. Kohlberg's (Kohlberg et al. 1974) notion of a "just community"—

in which students would have a role in determining rules that affect them, such as discipline policies, and would consider those policies to be fair—may be particularly important for at-risk students because they often feel that they are treated unjustly.

2. Afford students the opportunity to make decisions about instructional strategies, resources, and evaluative measures, as well as objectives. This does not mean, as some fear, turning the class over to students. It does mean being attentive to how students learn and think. Teachers in elementary and secondary school classrooms have translated this sharing of control into such tried and true instructional strategies as the use of contract learning and individualized instructional processes. They can also translate sharing into such simple tactics as asking students about their preferences (at times—not always!): "How can we best learn this? Which areas of the novel would you like to focus on?" Kohl (1966) describes the use of many such inclusion strategies with sixth graders in Harlem, for whom the standard curriculum was initially meaningless.

At-risk students in the classrooms of one of the authors were better able to exercise such control when compared with those students who were used to high achievement as the result of playing the academic game: "Tell me what to memorize. I will master those facts and repeat them on a test when you tell me to." Some of the at-risk students, not good at this game playing, were better able to set goals for their own work because they were exercising some control—control heretofore kept entirely by the teacher.

Such opportunities for shared control might be more easily exercised within an alternative school setting, in which teachers and students spend more time in collaborative planning of the instructional program. However, they have also been used in traditional settings in which at-risk students, as well as higher achievers, want to be treated as significant persons who have a right to make certain decisions.

Goal Setting

One of the authors has experimented fairly extensively with an organized approach to sharing some control: providing students with opportunities to set reasonable, attainable goals for themselves within elementary and secondary school classrooms. What this involves is asking students about goals they set for themselves outside school, eliciting examples of the kinds of strategies they used to achieve these goals, and then asking students to identify worthwhile goals for achievement within a specific subject area. We have seen bored and otherwise alienated students say, "I just want to pass this course or the mid-term." This is reasonable.

144

What many students, not just at-risk learners, have difficulty with is designing viable strategies. Usually they say, "I'll just study more." Few students have a well-developed awareness of the wide variety of strategies available to them to achieve any goal. Therefore, they need coaching in the planning of strategies to achieve a goal (Pressley et al. 1987). This technique requires teachers to carefully monitor progress and evaluate final results so that students see the relationship between their efforts, interest, and commitment and the final outcome. This connection is so vital because too many children and youths attribute their successes and/or failures to luck, chance, or mere characteristics of the task. Indeed, Coleman (1966) found that at-risk urban students felt a lack of what he called "fate control": the belief that what you do now could affect your future.

One as-yet-untried variation on this goal-setting theme is to help youngsters determine significant goals for their lives beyond school and design effective strategies for their attainment. This might be an excellent way for them to begin to see how school can be a meaningful resource in the achievement of life goals (Marzano 1988). When these activities are done by everyone in the class in a collaborative fashion, they provide excellent opportunities for students to engage in the kinds of peer interaction that many researchers (Johnson and Johnson 1984) maintain will result in cognitive development.

Collaborative Problem Solving

The extent to which at-risk students are afforded opportunities to engage in collaborative problem solving may determine whether or not they become less disaffected with school. Goal setting provides one such opportunity. Others are afforded by the teacher who can use such strategies as Whimbey and Lochhead's (1982) "paired problem solving" strategy, which fosters thinking aloud because it improves the quality of students' thinking. Elementary school teachers have used collaborative problem solving extensively with students at all grade levels and in all subjects (including physical education and special education); such experiences empower students to generate their own problem-solving rules. For example, students can figure out how a character in a novel can deal with a dilemma; they can assume the role of Thomas Jefferson and analyze whether or not to purchase the Louisiana Territory; they can generate hypotheses to determine why a particular scientific experiment did not work; and they can plan, monitor, and evaluate strategies to solve complex mathematical problems. They can do all of these things collaboratively and then, most significantly, reflect upon their own thinking by posing such questions as these:

- What was the problem?

145

- How did we solve it? (focus upon intellectual processes and emotional supports and/or blocks)
- Did we solve it well? (focus upon criteria)
- What would we do differently and why? (Barell, Liebmann, and Sigel 1988)

Responding to such questions ultimately empowers students to take more control of their own learning (Costa 1984).

A variation on the above strategy is to encourage students to recognize how they go about identifying and solving problems in their lives beyond school walls. Many of the disaffected and alienated students sitting in our classrooms have myriads of ways of solving problems. True, some of them are what Resnick (1987) has called "buggy algorithms." But some of these strategies probably would be effective in helping these same students become more successful in our classrooms.

Collaboration in problem solving is natural and productive in the world of business (Waterman and Peters 1982). Observation tells us that people collaborate to solve many problems outside the classroom, whether they are doctors diagnosing a patient with an acute illness or builders and architects trying to figure out how to match a plan to the realities of the building in front of them. Collaboration may be very productive because of how our minds function—not as autocratic, linear, decision-making mechanisms, but more as interactive networks of 100 billion cells listening to and responding to each other (Maxwell 1987).

Metacognitive Awareness

The questions we, as thinkers, can pose before, during, and after our engagement with problem solving are designed to affect our control over our own thinking. This approximates a definition of metacognition as awareness and control of one's own thinking processes (Presseisen 1985). Why such a strategy would be effective with at-risk students should by now be obvious: by definition, they have little sense of competence within school; they are detached and unmotivated, and see little connection between their "real" lives and what goes on in school. Empowering all students with ways of planning their approach to a problem ("What is my problem? How will I solve it?"), monitoring their progress ("How well am I doing?"), and evaluating their success ("Have I finished? How well have I done?") should, ultimately, affect the conduct of their lives both in and out of school.

These questions can be actualized through a variety of instructional practices:

1. Using "think aloud" processes

146

2. Writing in thinking journals (Barell, Liebmann, and Sigel 1988)
3. Engaging in group problem solving and reflecting on progress and results
4. Analyzing goal-setting progress weekly
5. Modeling by teachers and other students.

At-risk students can exercise control over their own thinking and these strategies should help eliminate some of the disaffection they apparently feel toward school. The aim of these strategies, for at-risk as well as for all other students, is to empower them to become more self-directed.

Alternative Educational Experiences

Alternative educational experiences are probably more feasible within a structure such as a minischool or school-within-a-school arrangement. These structures often are established so teachers and students can collaboratively plan experiences that are more meaningful to at-risk students. Such planning results in greater control of the content of learning and its acquisition. Students can engage in work-related experiences, such as internships in business and industry, during which they learn about various careers. They can establish businesses of their own, such as food co-ops or retail merchandising operations. And they can design opportunities to learn about the environment through outdoor education experiences—e.g., camping and horticulture.

All of these alternatives provide at-risk students with opportunities to learn about the world outside school. Such experiences remind us of Kilpatrick's once famous "Project Method" of learning. One of the similarities is that they give students a chance to integrate the learning of the fundamental or precedent skills of reading, writing, and computing, while engaging in complex and significant educational experiences. But these infusion strategies also afford at-risk students excellent opportunities to take greater control of both their educational and their personal lives. Beyond the goals of Kilpatrick's curriculum, we realize that if students work through these independent activities and are also challenged to reflect upon their own performance metacognitively, they may begin to design effective educational activities of their own.

QUALITY INSTRUCTION
AND A HEALTHY SCHOOL ENVIRONMENT

Providing a quality education that may constitute the best shot at-risk children have at a decent life after school requires more than the changes in classroom instructional processes outlined above. A classroom that fosters self-direction and improved awareness of the nature of critical thinking and problem solving will not survive very well unless it is in a thinking school. Furthermore, the alienation that students (and teachers) experience emanates from the whole school and its climate and policies. Teachers know, as do researchers, that the whole school organization must undergo alteration (Powell, Farrar, and Cohen 1985).

Decades of research on the nature of schooling have shown that although teachers and students envision their respective participation in school with delight and enthusiasm, once they are there, schools become downright enervating places (Sarason 1971). Both teachers and students complain of overwhelming feelings of powerlessness over their own thoughts and goals and of lack of control over their work. Both groups characterize schools as too impersonal, as places where students often feel invisible instead of cared about. Conformity is the standard of performance, and the atmosphere lacks trust. There is a pervasive feeling that pieces are being torn off of one's IALAC card. An IALAC card is that imaginary placard we all wear that says, "I Am Lovable And Capable'" (Simon 1973).

If we are to change the nature of schooling, we must examine and alter the very structure of our schools so that good thinking is an integral part of their fabric. We suggest that schools should be communities of growth and learning that enable students and faculty to reach their potential. This type of community requires a sense of collective responsibility (Lieberman 1987). Each person is responsible for his/her own learning, for that of others, and for the development and maintenance of an environment that enhances learning.

The fuel that drives such a community of shared decision making is careful, high-level, and collaborative thinking. Giving everyone in the school responsibility must be coupled with giving them training and support in thinking skills. For the school to function as a nurturing community based on collective responsibility, everyone must practice and model good thinking. Only through this kind of expectation can we ensure that the school operates primarily on a basis of reason and empathy.

Teachers as Leaders of School Reorganization

Who will take the lead in making these changes happen in schools? The goal of providing a quality education for all children in a healthy environment has spawned the current movement to restructure schools. Two major tenets of this restructuring are a focus on the needs of the whole child (Harvey and Crandall 1988) and a reformation of the roles and responsibilities of teachers (Carnegie Forum on Education 1986; Holmes Group 1986). Both are meant to empower students *and*

148

teachers—to give them power and control over their own lives through knowledge. The teaching of thinking as an explicit goal of education for every student is a major corollary of both these tenets.

One of the greatest challenges for teachers, as their roles are now redefined, is to be responsible simultaneously for classroom instruction and for shared leadership of the whole school. The editors of the *Harvard Educational Review* have recognized teachers as the most pivotal players in the educational enterprise (Anderson, Okazawa-Rey, and Traver 1986). The Carnegie and Holmes reports noted above are credited with fomenting discussions about teachers as change agents, central to influencing school workings in order to make them better places for students and faculty. The teacher as a thinker and as a model of thinking is a major player in the restructuring process.

The newly defined roles of teachers have three leadership aspects: leadership in restructuring the classroom, in realigning the curriculum, and in restructuring the whole school organization. Collectively, teachers are in a powerful position to have a perspective on the entire school workings; thus, they are able to be champions in producing knowledge as well as in producing a climate conducive to using that knowledge. Having *both* knowledge itself and a climate in which that knowledge is used and valued is necessary to empower teachers and students.

An environment that fosters thinking is characterized by certain significant pedagogical elements. These include setting up high expectations, modeling, questioning, wait time, nonjudgmental responding, generating peer interaction, a spirit of cooperation, transfer, and metacognitive awareness. Some of these elements, such as nonjudgmental responding, constitute a dramatic change in traditional instruction. Teacher educators must provide examples and models of these pedagogical strategies so teachers begin to feel comfortable in using them.

Bacon's adage that "Knowledge is power" may be true for an individual who is knowledgeable and feels privately powerful, but here we are discussing creating a school environment that attends simultaneously to private or personal power and to organizational empowerment. Pedagogical knowledge alone will not prepare teachers for their new roles as leaders of school change. They must have knowledge of the school organization and how it works in order to ensure the existence of a healthy school environment in which adults and children can learn.

Dimont (1971) provides an example that will dramatize this lesson that only the *freedom* to exercise knowledge, in combination with *knowledge* itself, is true power. He theorizes that many Jews prize education because they have been an oppressed people for a long time, able to enjoy few freedoms. They spent a great deal of time in pursuit of knowledge through reading and debate. But while these scholars acquired a great deal of knowledge, they had to hide themselves away to obtain it. Some Jewish scholars would probably not consider themselves powerful because, although brilliant, they did not enjoy the freedom to exercise their knowledge. Having knowledge in an environment that does not value that knowledge is like being rich in a currency one cannot spend.

EMPOWERING TEACHERS AS LEADERS

The school organization must be structured to encourage teachers to use their knowledge to work toward positive change in the school. An environment that fosters collaborative teacher, supervisor, and administrator planning for instructional and organizational improvement is essential. This mutual planning process will affect how we teach for thinking in the classroom, as well as the nature of the organization of the school.

Teaching critical reasoning in the classroom alone is not sufficient; this process will be facilitated by providing teachers with opportunities to pose and resolve problems that will result in certain changes in the structure of the entire school. Teachers' entrée into leadership roles is their expertise in the pedagogical, or teaching and learning, domain. Teachers will participate with administrators in long-range, three-to-five-year staff development processes that focus on identifying and resolving instructional and curricular problems. These problems could naturally focus on at-risk students as well as on the average or the gifted. In these processes we will see how teachers become engaged in collaboration, goal setting, and reflection on their own thinking. Here is where the interactive, dynamic aspects of our proposed process become most evident.

With a facilitative leader, teachers can be leaders, not only in instructional change but also in planning for organizational change by knowing how to strategize, set goals, evaluate progress, and redesign programs and policies based on evaluation results (Lieberman 1987).

Gideonse (1983) supports the importance of establishing a school-wide expectation of involvement in decision making and problem solving. Systematic and reflective inquiry ought to become the underlying professional frame of mind that guides teachers, administrators, teacher educators, and policy officials in the daily conduct of their responsibilities, he maintains. If administrators and teachers engage in systematic inquiry as they go about their planning and goal setting, their reflection will have a most powerful impact on teachers' ability to do the following:

1. Become more aware of their own thinking processes.
2. Be able to model these processes for their students using strategies

suggested above. Practice problem solving will, it is hoped, enable teachers to manifest more flexible thinking with at-risk students—encouraging *them* similarly to seek alternative solutions.

3. Have a definitive impact on the quality of communications in the school, the way in which instructional problems are posed and resolved, the realignment of the curriculum, and the design and implementation of long-range professional development plans.

That we believe teachers must play a pivotal role in school reform is not to say that teachers should constantly be distracted from what they love most—teaching. And, certainly, most teachers are clear that they do not want to be responsible for the daily management of the school. However, for teachers to make well-informed, responsible decisions about teaching and learning, they need to understand the impact their actions have on the whole school. Furthermore, teachers should have a voice in decisions about the leadership structure of the school, the roles and responsibilities of the faculty, the physical plant, the school's relationship to the community and to parents, and the school's various policies that affect students. These voiced decisions may result from long-range planning that focuses on instructional improvement. As teachers collaborate with each other and with administrators, they are exercising and reflecting on the patterns of control to be modeled with their at-risk students.

We are not suggesting that teachers become experts in everything and take over the responsibilities of the principalship. We cannot rebuild many schools from the ground up. In some schools, change will require a unified peer effort by administrators and faculty; in others, change will be initiated by the teachers or it will not happen at all. Lieberman (1987) wonders if "it is possible to conceive of principals and teachers moving away from the parent/child relationship to a far more collaborative, shared view, where principals and teachers can all be leaders in the school."

CONCLUSION

In this chapter, we have argued that our educational system suffers from systematic problems involving the very structure of our schools; they are evidenced by the dissatisfaction and nonproductivity of many students and teachers. These students and teachers share similar feelings that school does not meet their needs and that the school environment is one in which they feel powerless to perform at their best. This is all the more true for at-risk youngsters. The problem has manifested itself in large numbers of students dropping out of school or working well beneath their potential. This phenomenon has had a domino effect on teachers' sense of efficacy and pride.

In order to address this major restructuring for students and teachers, we propose a strategy for turning schools around that is undergirded by the advocacy of teaching and practicing thinking. In our vision, the whole school organization, including each individual classroom, could become a place of active engagement if each participant could control the decision making, problem posing and resolution, goal setting, and metacognitive awareness of their own thinking. Teachers would dramatically change their instruction to integrate thinking into the regular subject-matter lessons and would assume new roles as leaders of school change. They could model sound thinking practices.

DISCUSSION QUESTIONS

1. What is the concept of *content infusion* in teaching thinking, and how does such an approach seem to address the school learning problems of at-risk students?

2. What relationship seems to exist between a teacher's perception of self-efficacy and the achievement of his/her students?

3. How do shared leadership and collaborative effort influence the new empowered view of teaching? How does this view relate to making at-risk students more independent learners?

REFERENCES

American Association of State Colleges and Universities. 1986. *To secure the blessings of liberty.* Washington, D.C.: the Association.

Anderson, B. L., and Cox, P. L. 1988. *Configuring the education system for a shared future: Collaborative vision, action, reflection.* Andover, Mass.: Regional Laboratory for Educational Improvement of the Northeast and Islands; Denver: The Education Commission of the States.

Anderson, J.; Okazawa-Rey, M.; and Traver, R., eds. 1986. Teachers, teaching, and teacher education. Special Issue. *Harvard Educational Review* 56(4): v.

ASCD Task Force on Increased High School Graduation Requirements. 1985. *With consequences for all.* Alexandria, Va.: Association for Supervision and Curriculum Development.

Ashton, P. T., and Webb, R. B. 1986. *Making a difference.* White Plains, N. Y.: Longman.

Barell, J., ed. 1988. *Opening the American mind—Reflection on teaching thinking in higher education.* Upper Montclair, N.J.: Montclair State College.

Barell, J.; Liebmann, R.; and Sigel, I. 1988. Fostering thoughtful self-direction in students. *Educational Leadership* 45(7): 14–17.

Beekman, N., ed. 1987. The dropout's perspective on leaving school. *Highlights*. An ERIC/CAPS Digest. Ann Arbor, Mich.: Counseling and Personnel Services Clearinghouse.

Bennett, W. J. 1988. *American education: Making it work*. Washington, D.C.: U.S. Department of Education.

Berman, P., and McLaughlin, M. W. 1978. Federal programs supporting educational change. Vol. VIII, *Implementing the sustaining innovations*. Santa Monica, Calif.: Rand Corporation.

Brophy, J., and Good, T. L. 1984. *Teacher behavior and student achievement*. Occasional Paper no. 73. East Lansing, Mich.: Institute for Research on Teaching.

Cannon, E. H.; Costello, K.; LaPlante, P. O.; and Matulaitis, J. J. 1988. Teacher empowerment: Complex question with no simple answers. *MTA Today*, p. 2.

Carnegie Forum on Education and the Economy. 1986. *A nation prepared: Teachers for the 21st century*. Report of the Task Force on Teaching as a Profession. Washington, D.C.: the Forum.

Clifford, G. J., and Guthrie, J. W. 1988. Strategies for reforming schools of education. *Education Week* 4(37): 32.

Clinton, H. R. 1984. Teacher education: Of the people, by the people, and for the people. Austin, Tex.: Southwest Educational Developmental Laboratory.

Cohen, C. B. 1988. Teaching about ethnic diversity. *ERIC Digest*. No. 32. ERIC Document Service no. ED273539.

Coleman, J. S. 1966. *Equality of educational opportunity*. Washington, D.C.: U.S. Government Printing Office.

Commission for Educational Quality. 1985. *Improving teacher education: An agenda for higher education and the schools*. Atlanta: Southern Regional Education Board.

Costa, A. 1984. Mediating the metacognitive. *Educational Leadership* 42(3): 57–67.

Crandall, D. P., et al. 1982. *People, policies, and practices: Examining the chain of school improvement*. Andover, Mass.: The NETWORK, Inc.

Cruickshank, D. R. 1984. *Models for the preparation of America's teachers*. Bloomington, Ind.: Phi Delta Kappa Educational Foundation.

Darling-Hammond, L. 1984. *Beyond the commission reports: The coming crisis in teaching*. Santa Monica, Calif.: Rand Corporation.

Darling-Hammond, L. 1988. On the "cult of efficiency" in schools. *Education Week*.

Denton, J.; Peters, W.; and Savage, T., eds. 1984. *New directions in teacher education: Foundations, curriculum, policy*. College Station: Instructional Research Laboratory, College of Education, Texas A&M University.

Dimont, M. I. 1971. *The indestructible Jews*. New York: Signet Books.

Education Commission of the States and the Metropolitan Life Foundation. 1986. *Focusing the debate for positive change in teacher education*. Vol. 1 (Racine, Wisc.: Wingspread Conference Center). Denver: the Commission.

Education Commission of the States and the Metropolitan Life Foundation. 1986. *Focusing the debate for positive change in teacher education*. Vol. 2 (Tampa, Fla.). Denver: the Commission.

Egbert, R. L., and Kluender, M. M., eds. 1984. *Using research to improve teacher education: The Nebraska consortium*. Lincoln, Neb.: Clearinghouse on Teacher Education.

Eisner, E. 1988. The ecology of schools. *Educational Leadership* 45(5): 24–29.

Feistritzer, C. E. 1984. *The making of a teacher*. Washington, D.C.: National Center for Education Information.

Feuerstein, R. 1980. *Instrumental enrichment: An intervention program for cognitive modifiability*. In collaboration with Y. Rand, M. B. Hoffman, and R. Miller. Baltimore, Md.: University Park Press.

Fullan, M. 1982. *The meaning of educational change*. New York: Teachers College Press.

Fullan, M., and Connelly, F. M. 1987. *Teacher education in Ontario: Current practice and options for the future*. Toronto: Teacher Education Review.

Futrell, M. H. 1986. *Restructuring teaching: A call for research*. Washington, D.C.: National Education Association.

Garrison, J. W. 1988. Democracy, scientific knowledge, and teacher empowerment. *Teachers College Record* 89(4): 487–504.

Gideonse, H. 1983. *In search of more effective service*. Cincinnati: S. Rosenthal and Co.

Glatthorn, A. A., and Newberg, N. A. 1984. A team approach to instructional leadership. *Educational Leadership* 41(5): 60–63.

Harvey, G., and Crandall, D. P. 1988. *A beginning look at the what and how of restructuring*. Andover, Mass.: Regional Laboratory for Educational Improvement of the Northeast and Islands.

Holmes Group. 1986. *Tomorrow's teachers, A report of the Holmes Group*. East Lansing, Mich.: the Group.

Houston, W. R., ed. 1985. *Mirrors of excellence*. Reston, Va.: Association of Teacher Educators.

Howland, M. J., ed. 1987. *Connecticut's common core of learning*. Hartford: Connecticut State Board of Education.

Huberman, M. 1987. Recruiting and selecting teachers for urban schools. *ERIC/CUE Urban Diversity Series* 95.

Hurd, S., et al. 1987. *Taking charge of change*. Alexandria, Va.: Association for Supervision and Curriculum Development.

Jenks, L. 1984. *Making our schools more effective, Proceedings of three state conferences*. San Francisco: Far West Laboratory for Educational Research and Development.

Johnson, D., and Johnson, R. 1984. *Circles of learning*. Alexandria, Va.: Association for Supervision and Curriculum Development.

Kenney, J. L., and Roberts, J. M. E. 1984. *Teachers as instructional leaders*. Philadelphia: Research for Better Schools.

Kohl, J. 1966. *Quality of educational opportunity*. Washington, D.C.: U.S. Office of Education.

Kohlberg, L., et al. 1974. *Just community approach to corrections: A manual, Part I*. Boston: Moral Education Research Foundation.

Landsmann, L. 1988. 10 resolutions for teachers. *Phi Delta Kappan* 69(5): 373–76.

Lazerson, M.; McLaughlin, J. B.; McPherson, B.; and Bailey, S. K. 1985. *An education of value*. Cambridge, England: Cambridge University Press.

Levin, H. M. 1987. Accelerated schools for disadvantaged students. *Educational Leadership* 44(6): 19–21.

Lieberman, A., ed. 1986. *Rethinking school improvement: Research, craft, and concept*. New York: Teachers College Press.

Lieberman, A. 1987. Expanding the leadership team in schools: From isolation to participation. Paper presented at the NSDC Conference, Seattle.

Lieberman, A., and Miller, L. 1984. *Teachers, their world, and their work*. Alexandria, Va.: Association for Supervision and Curriculum Development.

Loucks-Horsley, S., and Hergert, L. F. 1985. *An action guide to school improvement*. Alexandria, Va.: Association for Supervision and Curriculum Development.

McDonald, J. P. 1988. The emergency of the teacher's voice: Implications for the new reform. *Teachers College Record* 89(45): 471–86.

Mace-Matluck, B. J. 1986. *Research-based tools for bringing about successful school improvement*. Austin, Tex.: Southwest Educational Development Laboratory.

Maeroff, G. I. 1988. A blueprint for empowering teachers. *Phi Delta Kappan* 69(7): 472–77.

March, E., et al., eds. 1986. *The Bar Harbor colloquium on teacher education*. New York: Academy for Educational Development.

Marzano, R. 1988. Practicing theory. *Cogitare* 2(4): 5–6.

Maxwell, W. 1987. Human brain as model for decision making. In *Thinking: The second international*, ed. D. N. Perkins, J. Lochhead, and J. C. Bishop. Hillsdale, N.J.: Lawrence Erlbaum Associates.

Mayer, R. 1975. Information processing variables in learning to solve problems. *Review of Educational Research* 45:525–42.

Mirman, J., and Tishman, S. 1988. Infusing thinking through "Connections." *Educational Leadership* 45(7): 64–65.

Mojkowski, C., and Fleming, D. 1988. *School-site management: Concepts and approaches*. Providence: Rhode Island Educational Leadership Academy.

National Governors Association Center for Policy Research and Analysis. 1986. *Time for results: The governors' 1991 report on education*. Washington, D.C.: the Association.

Newcombe, E., ed. 1987. *Perspectives on teacher induction: A review of the literature and promising program models*. Baltimore: Maryland State Department of Education Staff Development Branch and Research for Better Schools.

Newmann, F. M. 1987. Higher order thinking in the teaching of social studies: Connections between theory and practice. Paper presented at a conference on informal reasoning and education, Learning Research and Development Center, University of Pittsburgh.

Olson, L. 1988. A Seattle principal defies the conventional wisdom. *Education Week*.

Pellicano, R. 1987. At risk: A view of social advantage. *Educational Leadership* 44(6): 47–49.

Perkins, D. N. 1986. Thinking frames. *Educational Leadership* 43(8): 4–10.

Perkins, D. N. 1987. Myth and method in teaching thinking. *Teaching Thinking and*

Problem Solving 9(2): 1, 2, 8, 9.

Pierce, O. 1986. *No easy roses.* Boston: Thomas Todd Company.

Powell, A. G.; Farrar, E.; and Cohen, D. K. 1985. *The shopping mall high school.* Boston: Houghton Mifflin.

Presseisen, B. Z. 1985. Thinking skills: Meanings and models. In *Developing minds: A resource book for teaching thinking,* ed. A. L. Costa, 43–48. Alexandria, Va.: Association for Supervision and Curriculum Development.

Pressley, M., et al. 1987. What is good strategy use and why is it hard to teach? Paper presented at the annual meeting of the American Educational Research Association, Washington, D.C.

Research for Better Schools. 1988. At-risk youth: Some answers. *RBS Project Brief* 5:1–4.

Resnick, L. B. 1987. *Education and learning to think.* Washington, D.C.: National Academy Press.

Sarason, S. B. 1971. *The culture of the school and the problem of change.* Boston: Allyn & Bacon.

Sedlak, M., and Schlossman, S. 1986. Who will teach? In *Historical perspectives on the changing appeal of teaching as a profession.* Santa Monica, Calif.: Rand Corporation.

Simon, S. B. 1973. *The IALAC story.* Niles, Ill.: Argus Communications.

Slavin, R. E. 1981. Synthesis of research on cooperative learning. *Educational Leadership* 38(8): 655–60.

Smith, D. C. 1983. *Essential knowledge for beginning educators.* Washington, D.C.: American Association of Colleges for Teacher Education/ERIC Clearinghouse on Teacher Education.

Smith, E. D., ed. 1978. *Teacher education developmental profiling, A handbook.* Austin: The University of Texas at Austin/Austin Independent School District Eleventh Cycle Teacher Corps Program.

Smith, S. C., ed. 1986. New structures build collaboration among teachers and administrators. *OSSC Report* 27(1): 1–7.

Swartz, R. J. 1986. Restructuring curriculum for critical thinking. *Educational Leadership* 43(8): 43–44.

Wassermann, S. 1987. Teaching for thinking: Louis E. Raths revisited. *Phi Delta Kappan* 68(6): 460–66.

Waterman, R. H., and Peters, T. J. 1982. *In search of excellence.* New York: Warner Books.

Wehlage, G. G., and Rutter, R. A. 1986. Evaluation of a model program for at-risk high school students. Paper presented at the annual meeting of the American Educational Research Association, San Francisco.

Whimbey, A., and Lochhead, J. 1982. *Problem solving and comprehension.* Philadelphia: Franklin Institute Press.

THE CONTRIBUTORS

John Barell is Associate Professor of Curriculum at Montclair State College. His particular interests include teaching thinking and staff development. For the past four years he has headed the Network on Teaching Thinking for the Association for Supervision and Curriculum Development.

Richard P. Durán is Associate Dean, Graduate Division of the University of California at Santa Barbara, and Associate Professor in the Educational Psychology program. He has written extensively on significant predictors of college achievement for Spanish-speaking students, and he is interested in both the theory and the practice of problem solving in the context of verbal ability and language proficiency.

Beau Fly Jones is Program Director at the North Central Regional Educational Laboratory. Well known as an author and editor, she is a primary developer of the program *Teaching Reading as Thinking*. She is particularly interested in the development of strategic instruction and the implications of such an innovation in the restructuring of elementary and secondary schools.

Daniel U. Levine is Professor of Education and Director of the Center for the Study of Metropolitan Problems in Education at the University of Missouri. He has written widely on topics ranging from institutional change to mastery learning. Currently he is focusing on reading and language instruction with particular implications for organizational strategy and policy.

Jill A. Mirman is Program Coordinator for Teacher Development at the Regional Laboratory for Educational Improvement of the Northeast and Islands. She coordinates the development of the Connections project, aimed at helping teachers reshape instruction so that they routinely infuse the teaching of thinking into all content areas.

Barbara Z. Presseisen is Director of National Networking at Research for Better Schools, the mid-Atlantic educational laboratory. For the past three years she has chaired the Cross-Laboratory Committee for Higher Order Thinking Skills. Her writings and publications focus on school reform, innovations in curriculum and instruction, and the significance of cognitive development in planning and implementing school programs.

157

Trevor E. Sewell is a school psychologist and well-known researcher on learning ability and intelligence assessment in minority populations. He serves as Associate Dean for Academic Affairs at Temple University's College of Education. He is particularly interested in aspects of dynamic assessment associated with research on Reuven Feuerstein's *Instrumental Enrichment* program and with related issues of cognitive modifiability.

Robert J. Swartz is the founder of the Critical and Creative Thinking Program at the University of Massachusetts, Boston Harbor Campus. For the past several years he has concentrated his efforts on helping teachers understand and implement an infusion approach to integrating the teaching of thinking into the content areas.

OPERATION RESCUE

Each year more than one million children and young adults drop out of schools or are chronically truant. The consequences of dropping out, for both our nation and the individuals involved, are staggering. Dropouts are more likely to be unemployed than their graduate counterparts. When they are employed, dropouts earn approximately one-third less. Dropouts are more likely to be the parents of the next generation's underclass, and they tend to be overrepresented in our nation's prisons. The impact of dropping out on the lives of these children and on the future of our nation requires immediate, direct, and focused action.

Operation Rescue was created as a vehicle for initiating this action. In 1985, 1.7 million education professionals who are members of the National Education Association voted to contribute their own money to the National Foundation for the Improvement of Education (NFIE) to launch a national assault on the dropout crisis. For the first two years, $700,000 was designated for dropout prevention grants and for years to come, $1 million was earmarked to begin NFIE's endowment to make educational excellence grants available to teachers.

Operation Rescue is a multifaceted program. It centers on a strategy aimed at direct action and practical solutions. It includes grant giving, information exchanges, publications, and dissemination of results.

By continuing to build on the momentum that Operation Rescue has established, NFIE will further advance the empowerment of teachers, the restructuring of schools to improve education for all students, and the opportunity for each student to realize his or her full potential. This will enable students to have the knowledge, skills, and confidence to meet the challenges that they will face, and those that society will face in the future.

For further information contact:

THE NATIONAL FOUNDATION
FOR THE IMPROVEMENT OF EDUCATION
1201 16th Street, NW, Washington DC 20036 (202) 822-7840

A Joint Publication of
National Education Association
   1201 16th Street, N.W., Washington, DC 20036–3290
Research for Better Schools
   444 North Third Street, Philadelphia, PA 19123–4107